Music Therapy Group Vignettes

MUSIC THERAPY:
Group Vignettes

Ronald M. Borczon

Barcelona PUBLISHERS

WM
450.5
.M8
B726m
1997

ISBN 0-962080-7-7
Library of Congress Card Number

2 4 6 8 9 7 5 3

Distributed throughout the world
by
Barcelona Publishers
4 Whitebrook Road
Gilsum, NH 03448
800-345-6665

Cover design by Frank McShane

PRINTED IN THE UNITED STATES OF AMERICA

TABLE OF CONTENTS

FOREWORD

While working with clients in the music therapy experience, I have seen countless mini-miracles occur and many "light bulbs" illuminate over the head of self-actualizing individuals. As a music therapist, I have not come to take these events for granted. I have found that each is unique in character, individualized, meaningful and at times life-changing for the person. It is difficult to document these personal events except in progress notes that other professionals may read. The documentation really lies in the imprint of the session on the clients as they use it on their journey to a better place labeled health. The clients are the best voices to validate the effectiveness of music therapy.

Before the actual chapters containing the vignettes, I offer some of my concepts regarding the qualities of a music therapist, music therapy, and strategies for intervention. I hope that you find these valuable, as I think they prepare you for how I use music in a group therapy setting. These first four chapters may be particularly helpful for young therapists with little experience.

After the first four chapters come the vignettes, each coupled with a preceding chapter that is philosophical in nature. The philosophical background of each vignette lays the groundwork to launch new and creative music therapy interventions as well as being the foundation for the following vignette.

The names of the clients that are used in the vignettes are fictional, but the stories are not. The dialogue was recalled immediately after a session and written down as well as I could remember. You will read references to the power of the music therapy session as recounted by the clients and, at times, their appreciation of the therapist. As the therapist, I see my role often as the bringer of the music. The music has the power, and I am there to be Present for the client; to be available and serve in many different capacities.

As you read the vignettes, you will see that there are *italicized* sections that are separated from the dialogues. These are my thoughts during the session. They are my internal reflections about what I think is happening and perhaps what I should do next. The sections in parentheses are observations of behavior or factual information that is pertinent to that particular part of the vignette.

The stories that follow are not complete histories of the clients' treatment. They are, rather, moments taken from the journey through therapy of many individuals. They illustrate important events in the therapeutic group process. As you read I hope that you can envision the session, get a feeling of the structure, and try to hear—through your reading, the voices of the clients sharing their experience of music therapy. From this point, you can then see the importance of the session as part of a treatment process. These sessions are the links in the chain that are too often overlooked when viewing an entire case study.

Music is a potent force in life. It can portray all the emotional labels we currently can provide. It is most powerful when it resonates with the soul—when it reverberates the very nature on which we base our actions. In this way, it is God's special gift to us. What is most lacking in this book is that I can't bring the music to you that the clients experienced. I can only tell you about it. But I have faith that there has been a time in your life when music has moved you to tears or to joy. So, even though you cannot hear the sounds I offered them or those which they created, I sense that your musical imagination can be a substitute for the real music.

DEDICATION

To my children Jordyn, Claire, and Molly,
I am blessed for having you all in my life.
And to my mom Julia,
Who loved me unconditionally.

ACKNOWLEDGMENTS

In the writing of this book I have saved this to write last, even though these may be the first words that you read. This writing has been a labor of love and is a compilation of many years of working with people who are going through changes. They are courageous individuals, who allowed me the honor of bringing music to them in order to aid them and at times, guide them. I could have not done this without the help, support, encouragement, and faith of several people.

Thanks to Dr. Ken Bruscia. He urged me to write this work instead of the one I thought I needed to write. He was right! He has also been the most inspirational teacher, friend, colleague, guide, and role model.

Thanks to Carolyn Braddock, I learned more than you'll ever know by watching you work—you are one of a kind.

Thanks to my brother Norman for all your e-mails asking me when is it going to be finished.

Thanks to Jim Dziwak, Michael Chapdelaine, Gino Ferrare, and Ron Purcell—you all personify the word "friend."

Thanks to Dr. Gerard Kneiter for the hours of reading, corrections and encouragement. Your philosophical discussions gave me food for thought.

I want to thank God, for being my Heavenly Father, for His guidance and love.

And finally to my sister Gloria, thanks for all those years when I was little—and you were there.

Music Therapy Group Vignettes

Chapter 1

PRELUDE

I love music for all that it makes me remember, all that it makes me forget, but most importantly, for all that it is.

I was driving on the freeway in the early evening. From my car stereo, Stravinsky's "Firebird Suite" was ending, the triumphal final moments of music exploding as the full moon shone through the fog ahead of me. I thought of how so many of my clients have told me in therapy sessions that as they listened to this music they imagined a grand sunrise. They had visions of castles rising out of the mist of morning dew, a sense of the brand new day and new beginnings. And there I was, on a freeway, remembering these thoughts. The moon slipped in and out through the fog in front of me like a beacon. The grandeur of the music had a full crescendo and filled a space moving 62 miles per hour. I then caught myself whispering, "It figures . . ."

My next thoughts came upon me suddenly, as thoughts often do when they have a beacon. They were thoughts I have had before, but not with as much clarity. What is it like to experience Music Therapy for the first time? What will clients remember? What will they feel? What is their perception of the therapist? Can this musical experience become like a sunrise ending the darkest point of the evening? Or maybe it could give them a glimmer of moonlight while following the path of discovery.

Understanding the sense of the client's perspective is all-important. Being in touch, in sync, in tune with clients shows them a doorway for their first session. The music then opens the door, and you must be available on the other side for them, with a sense of presence, intuition, knowledge, common sense, and a flashlight of sound, so that they can find their way. I have found these five things can allow clients to move in directions that they thought they could never move. They can explore new ways of looking at the world, which are stimulated by unique musical experiences. The music therapist who possesses presence, intuition, knowledge, and common sense, becomes the guide into and through the experience. As you read about these qualities, take note of how they relate to you, and how you can increase your personal ability to focus and refine these qualities for the betterment of your clients.

PRESENCE

I am in the present. I cannot know what tomorrow will bring forth. I can know only what the truth is for me today. That is what I am called upon to serve, and I serve it in all lucidity.

—Igor Stravinsky (1936)

I have supervised many students who are learning to be music therapists and have observed many types of therapists in clinical practice. Early in my career I began to ask to the question —what is **IT** that makes one a good therapist? Even better, what is **IT** that makes one a good music therapist. One of the most important factors is being Present for your clients. When I say this, I am thinking of *Being Present* on two different levels. One meaning of "present" is that which is happening now, being self-possessed, collected, ready to act or assist. You are paying attention to all the verbal, physical and musical cues that the client is offering to you. Clients will often respond at some point during or after the session that they felt that you were really "with them." When this occurs, we can look at the other meaning of "present," which is what we refer to as a gift! When we give someone a present, we are giving him something as an extension of ourselves. Our Presence (an extension of ourselves) is thus a gift for the other person. From this, they can find the feelings of security and trust; we become a confidant and are with them so they can be free to explore and express. Presence can also refer to the atmosphere you create for the music therapy session. Your Presence creates the atmosphere, and in this sense it can also become a gift for the client, for things often are given in music therapy that are not given in other more traditional talk therapies. Grant Rudolph (1988) says:

> This presence heals. Name it the transcendent function, God, the Self, the urge of the psyche to

individuate, or the archetypes; when this invisible guest is in the room, its presence cannot be denied. This presence is evoked by music. Like the star that it is so faint it can not be detected by the direct gaze of the human eye's focal point, but only when we look beside it and let its light fall on the more sensitive cones of the eye, this presence blesses us when our conscious focus shifts sideways. While hearing music, something moves, a boundary is crossed, the invisible guest arrives. (P. 68)

One way the client may perceive Presence is when they feel and experience empathy from the therapist. Rogers (1980) defines empathy as follows:

It means entering the private world of the other and becoming thoroughly at home in it. It involves being sensitive, moment by moment, to the changing felt meanings which flow in this other person, to the fear or rage or tenderness or confusion or whatever he or she is experiencing. It means temporarily moving in the other's life, moving about in it delicately without making judgments. (P. 142)

When the client senses empathy, it can increase the possibilities for open expression and advance the healing process. Rogers views this as so powerful that in itself, it is often a condition that helps the client progress.

To my mind, empathy itself is a healing agent. It is one of the most potent aspects of therapy, because it releases, it confirms, it brings even the most frightened client into the human race. If a person is understood, he or she belongs. (Rogers, 1986, P. 129)

I think it is important to understand this basic concept of Rogers and not confuse it with sympathy. Sympathy leans more toward a sense of having compassion and pity. Empathy is truly sensing what the other is experiencing, and through this process, trust can be established. Empathy comes first with the attitude of the therapist. It is a Presence that is available. Sympathy is given. Empathy is a resonance of the other's feeling state. When the client comes into the room, the attitude that the therapist should have is one of honor for this person. For it is honorable to have someone enter and offer to us all that they are and to trust us with that. So the least and, often most, we can do is be Present for them, and with that, to show empathy.

INTUITION

It is the heart that always sees, before the head can see.

—Thomas Carlyle (1839)

Intuition is the immediate knowing or learning of something without the conscious use of reasoning. It is a spontaneous inner voice that says, "This way." Intuition is that aspect of being a therapist that enables one to say or do something not because one has mastered a specific technique, but because one just knows. It helps guide the therapeutic process and many other aspects of our life. It is often thought of being based on experience and knowledge stored at an unconscious level. From there, it can be called upon in an immediate fashion to lead the way to consciousness. Intuition is innate in all of us, yet seemingly rarely recognized and discussed. Understanding that one has this valuable resource empowers the therapist by helping the clients to rely on their own intuition.

Eugene Pascal (1992) says this about the relationship of intuition to the senses:

> We perceive reality with our sensation function, using our five senses—sight, sound, smell, taste, and touch. We may also perceive reality with a "sixth sense" called intuition. With sensation we see corners, but with intuition we see around corners. With sensation we can only see the lines as they are printed in black and white. With intuition we can read between the lines. (P. 16)

How do you know if you possess it? Think of all the times you should have gone with your first choice, but didn't, and later said, "I should have gone with my first choice." Intuition is that part of us that leads us instinctively. As we grow older, it seems that the sense of intuition becomes more refined. We seek the knowledge of those who are older, who have often survived not by just knowledge, but also through intuition.

KNOWLEDGE

Any piece of knowledge that I acquire today has a value at this moment exactly proportioned to my skill to deal with it. Tomorrow, when I know more, I will recall that piece of knowledge and use it better.

—Mark Van Doren (1960)

Knowledge is having a clear perception of an idea or something tangible, understanding its facets. Knowledge refers to a sense of intelligence that one can acquire something new, retain it, and hopefully apply it in a practical manner.

There are different types of knowledge. One is "book" knowledge – that which we primarily acquire through educational process. Through the learning of personality theory and treatment techniques, we acquire a foundation for developing counseling skills. The base is important because it forms the structure for our approach to the client. It gives us keys as to why the client may do the things he does, as well as what thought processes may be behind such behaviors. This foundation also gives us a road map that we try to share with the client through musical experiences, so they can continue on the path to health.

New experiences, or experiential knowledge, are extremely valuable and can do many things for us. Two that I feel are important are development of our skills and the opportunity to expand our base of knowledge. As the knowledge base grows, so too does our outlook of the world. Our philosophy of life is intricately involved with our growth. Jung (1928) says, "Every increase in our experience and knowledge means a further step in our 'philosophy of life.' And with the image the thinking man makes of the world, he also changes himself." (P.470)

Developing self-knowledge is a life-long task. It is important not only to understand what the client brings to the session, but also what we ourselves bring to it. It is necessary to fully understand our own assumptions, beliefs, values, standards, skills, strengths, weaknesses, idiosyncrasies, style of doing things, foibles, and temptations (Egan 1990). All these have a way of permeating our interaction with our clients.

Part of self-knowledge is understanding why you are there. Meir (1989, P.55) offers the following questions to those who wish to engage in the helping profession:

1. How did you decide to be a helper?
2. Why did you decide to be a helper?
3. With what emotions are you comfortable?
4. What emotions-in yourself or in others give you trouble?
5. What are your expectations of clients?
6. How will you deal with your clients' feelings toward you?
7. How will you handle your feelings toward your clients?
8. To what degree can you be flexible? accepting? gentle?

We must continue on our own journey of development. When we do, we bring to the client our own personal knowledge, wisdom, and a personal philosophy of life. Clients are often so lost that they hope that someone will show them the right path. We as therapists know, however, that ultimately our lost clients will eventually choose their own paths, and we merely help illuminate the alternatives.

COMMON SENSE

Good intentions are useless in the absence of common sense.

-JAMI (15th c.)

Common sense relies on standard conventions of the world, practical phrases, and acceptable modes of behavior. To have good common sense is an asset in any field, but even more so for the world of the therapist.

Phrases such as "never burn your bridges" or "treat someone as you would like to be treated" are verbal examples of common sense. I have found that phrases such as these may be spontaneously spoken by my clients. The phrase is usually rooted deep within their belief system and arises for some specific reason.

Common sense is a mediator between intuition and knowledge. It is there to be called upon on in a daily therapeutic situation, and also in daily life. Identify some of the people in your life who you believe have good common sense. Notice how they interact with others, how they solve mini-conflicts in life. Without common sense, a therapist often will not be able to maintain communication and trust with clients. The client may become alienated and uncertain of the relationship with the therapist.

For a therapist, common sense also has to do with basic factors of affect, voice tone, body language and therapeutic interaction. Imagine yourself in the client's position looking at your face. Is it accepting, flat, smiling, cynical? Is your voice tone harsh, rough, too loud or soft for the moment? Is the pacing of your questions too fast or slow? Is body language open, or do you sit with arms and legs tightly crossed? What are some of the basic features that you would like to see in your therapist if you were a client? After you identify those features, you might say, it's common sense to have them.

SUMMARY

As I watch young therapists grow and mature in their practice, the elements of presence, intuition, knowledge, and common sense should also be growing. Intuition and common sense are much more innate and come more from a natural process as the therapist himself develops as a person. Knowledge develops through life experience as well as from learning more about the art of therapy. Presence is not only the culmination of the previous three, but also in itself, a healing principle.

In using music as an integral element of the therapeutic environment, the atmosphere for healing and change increases. The client is involved in a creative and artistic process that allows for new avenues for self-discovery and growth.

REFERENCES

Egan, G. (1990). *The skilled helper: A systematic approach to effective helping.* Pacific Grove, CA: Brooks/Cole Publishing Company.

Jung, C. G. (1928). "The Swiss Line in the European Spectrum." Vol 10, (June 1928) pp. 469–479. *The collected works of C. G. Jung.* Princeton, NJ: Princeton University Press.

Meier, S. & S. Davis. (1993). *The elements of counseling.* Pacific Grove, CA: Brooks/Cole Publishing Company.

Pascal, E. (1992). *Jung to live by: a guide to the practical application of Jungian principles for everyday life.* New York: Warner Books.

Rogers, C. R. (1968). Reflection of feelings. *Person Centered Review, 2,* 375–377.

Rogers, C. R. (1968). The increasing involvement of the psychologist in social problems. *California State Psychologist,* 9:29.

Rogers, C. R. (1986). Rogers, Kohut, and Erickson. *Person Centered Review, 2,* 125–140.

Rogers, C. R. (1980). *A way of being.* Boston, MA: Houghton Mifflin.

Rudolph, G. (1988). Dreamsinging: sounding the depths of psychic images. Unpublished Master's Thesis. Human Relations Institute.

Chapter 2

MUSIC AND LIFE:
BASIC RELATIONSHIPS

*Take a music-bath once or twice a week for a few seasons, and you
will find that it is to the soul what the water-bath is to the body.*

—Oliver Wendell Holmes (1891)

I have referred to music as a beacon for our use. It can be held,
it can be turned on and off, and it has different degrees of intensity.
Most importantly, however, it can lead us and our clients through
the darkness. Sometimes we direct the beacon (music) for our
clients, and, at other times, they bravely take hold of it and explore.
Through music, there can be a resonance of their thoughts and
feelings. For many of the clients, words are not sufficient to
portray what they feel, so music becomes their mode of expression.
Through the musical expression, new roads are traveled, new
signposts seen, and answers come not only musically, but often
back to the spoken word. Thus a full circle is realized in the
process beginning with words, leaving the words to explore
musically, and then coming back to find the right words for verbal
processing. This circle of communication takes on tremendous
power in a music therapy group and enables clients to gain insight
so that they may move forward in their lives.

As I have grown as a music therapist, I have seen the dynamics
of this circle occur many times. I have truly begun to understand
how we are musical beings and how by getting in touch with and
understanding our music, we can grow as humans.

The elements of music are innate within us as a species.
Because of our interwoven relationship with music, we can easily
create musical vignettes that have personal meaning. We are
readily affected by and respond to music that is in our
environment. Through music therapy a relationship develops
between the client and music. In understanding the nature of this
relationship lies the key in opening doors not only to, but also for
the client.

MELODY

Music is a part of us, and either ennobles or degrades our behavior.

- Boethius (A.D. 6th c.)

Melody arises from the voice, and when it is elaborated, songs are created. In an effort to imitate the voice and to be more expressive, instruments were developed. Some instruments serve not only to imitate, but also accompany the voice. Speaking, singing, and playing can take on structure as if sentences are being sung. Thus, the concept of the question and answer as found in speech becomes evident in music. Whole conversations can develop, which lead to more complex songs and larger pieces of music.

The melody of a person's voice will often echo his emotional being. In therapy, the tone of the voice and its cadential factors are important in understanding the state of the client. Questions should be addressed such as: What musical descriptors can be used to analyze the voice? What does it mean when the voice sounds like a child, defensive, or angry? What kind of timbre in a voice makes it sound self-assured or scared to death? Does the content of what is said match how it is said and if not, why? These are the musical questions a music therapist must grapple with and understand. To establish trust, you may respond to your clients' melodies, and imitate their inflections. You might help them notice their vocal melodies as they relate to the content of what they say. When clients say something very significant, the manner in which they say it can become a basis for a whole musical improvisation or composition. As you understand what they give you from a verbal melodic perspective, you can begin to be in a place of being able to truly be present for the client.

Along with noticing the melodic inflections of the voice, you should also notice the aspect of silence, or rest as one speaks. Are they reflecting on what they just said? Do they need time to gather their thoughts together? Do they just need a break? Composers use silence very expressively. Musically, silence can be used to create tension, give time for resolution, allow time to breathe, create an opportunity or another instrument or voice to enter, or allow for a time of reflection. All these musical reasons for silence are the same reasons for silence in conversation.

TEXTURE

When you think of texture, you often think of something tangible, such as the feeling of a fabric, or the material something is made of. Musical texture is the sense of how something "feels" to the ear, the tangible sound. Texture refers to how complex the overall sense of sound is or to the "layers" of sound that one hears.

There are different types of texture in music. These types can be looked at both musically and in relationship to human behavior. When you think of a person's theme(s) in life, in one way you are looking at the texture of that life. If someone has one and only one theme that stands alone, it might be said that he has a monophonic thematic life. In music, monophonic is defined as "Music consisting of a single melodic line without additional parts or accompaniment . . . the purest realization of the melodic element" (Apel, 1972, P. 539). A person such as this may be so driven that he cannot see anything else around him. On the other hand, it may be a single simple theme that one follows as a rule, dogma, or guide through life. Such a life is entirely subject to the theme.

Many people have a homophonic texture, the musical definition of which is "Music in which one voice leads melodically, being supported in chordal or a slightly more elaborate style" (Apel, 1972, P. 390). One might think of popular music where you have a singer singing the melodic line, and the band "backs up" or supports the singer. A homophonic personality would have a basic belief system that is supported by the way in which he lives his life. Just as harmony supports a melodic line, so does the behavior of the client support his belief system. The theme may modulate through time, keeping the basic constructs, and the behaviors will adjust accordingly. This person is more open to change and growth than one who is monophonic, as mentioned earlier. If his behaviors and belief system are incongruent, internal problems will often arise for the person. He will sense "disharmony" in his life or a sense of not being grounded or supported.

Polyphonic music can be described as, "Music that combines several simultaneous voices—parts of individual design, in contrast to monophonic music, which consists of a single melody, or homophonic music, which combines several voice—parts of similar, rhythmically identical design" (Apel, 1972, P. 687). The implication is that more than one melody or theme is occurring at the same time. Each theme is trying to get the listeners' attention and can usually stand by itself as a theme. Polyphonic people have many themes, which at many times, are all of the same importance. They try to juggle all the things and emotions in their life. These people are often overworked and stressed, and while appearing tireless, they are emotionally and mentally fatigued.

Character types may often react strongly, either favorably or unfavorably, to the texture of music. I believe this reaction is important to notice, for it may be close to a certain issue or part of a belief structure. When clients can verbalize their reasons for this reaction, these verbalizations are often describing aspects of their life or thought processes. Thus texture can be used as a musical method of working with a client. When people talk about the texture of a piece of music, they speak from an internal frame of reference that is stimulated by and resonates with that texture.

FORM

Musical form is the way the themes of a piece are organized sequentially. The main purpose of form is to hold the large musical ideas of a composition together, so that the composition makes sense to the listener. Form organizes melodic and harmonic movement through time.

Life has different types of form. There are belief systems and themes that guide us through life, in essence organize it and give it form. Seconds, minutes, hours, days, months, seasons, years all have inherent form. In looking at some various musical forms, you can see how they are similar to life.

A rondo form is characterized by a theme that is stated several times in a piece of music, and between each statement, different musical material occurs. This pattern is represented by the letters ABACADA, with (A) representing the theme; and (B), (C), and

(D) being melodic departures from the theme. This theme (melody) is most often thought of as being contained within a homophonic structure. In life, there are main themes (behaviors) like that represented by the rondo letter (A). These themes can at times be interrupted by other life circumstances (B, C, and D in the rondo form); however, the themes keep returning, and are basically unchanged. The themes may be and often are supported by other behaviors (a sense of homophonic structure).

Fugue is similar to rondo in that a main theme is the organizing aspect of the piece, yet there are some important differences. The main theme of the fugue is called the subject. As a noun, "subject" is defined as a person or thing that is to be discussed or treated—the topic. As a verb, "subject" means to bring under control. Both definitions are important in the conceptual framework of the fugue. The subject not only is the main topic of the composition, but it also controls the composition in such a way that it is pervasive. It permeates the composition even when it is not audible in its complete statement.

The fugue subject is introduced as a monophonic melody. This subject is the main theme of the entire composition. As it concludes its statement, it continues to progress as a linear voice. The moment it concludes as a theme, one hears the theme again but at a different pitch level. This restatement of the theme now takes on a different name, the answer. Keep in mind that the original subject voice is now using different melodic material, either above or below this answer. Because of the nature of at least two voices or melodies simultaneously trying to exist, the texture now changes to polyphony, which means more complexity. This can continue until all the "voices" have made their statement of the theme, which is called the "exposition." Fugues generally have three or four voices (similar to that of a choir: soprano, alto, tenor, and bass). After these voices have made their statements, the piece continues in polyphonic texture. This continuation, is called an episode. The episode may take rhythmic or melodic pieces of the "subject" and develop them (and in essence the subject is still in control), or the episode may consist of new melodic material. At some point, the "subject" returns to be heard again, and this is called an "entry." The other voices, however, don't support this return as in a rondo. They continue on their own way trying to get the attention of the listener. Indeed, in some fugues, the sound is so complex it may be difficult to hear the subject restatement at all! Yet this subject, along with its subsequent bits and pieces throughout the fugue, is the main organizational factor of this form. Even trying to describe the workings of a fugue is a complicated matter, and one can easily become nonplused!

Similarly, at times in life, a person's themes can get very complex. The original theme of his life may become splintered, difficult to hear, yet in an underlying way it is a main issue in his life. In fact, the theme may become so repressed into the unconscious that it can barely be audible at all. Yet from this deep place, it controls all. This theme may be productive or not, depending on the personality. The main issue is that life has become complex, at times very difficult, and it is controlled by an underlying theme. In essence, the subject (noun) may have also subjected himself to certain styles of behavior. This type of form in one's life can be very destructive. As he engages in behaviors, which splinter his life, he cannot seem to consciously find the reason for these behaviors or even understand why he engages in them. His therapy is one of truly finding the main theme or subject that fuels the process.

There are many different types of form in music. The thematic content can be simply stated and restated; it can be stated, developed and returned to in either a simple or complex fashion; it can be stated and then never really returned to again. When looking at the form in life from a musical perspective, it sometimes is easier to understand what is going on and how to get to the theme. Improvisations and personal history compositions are excellent methods of helping the client understand the concept form in his life. Sometimes you can help structure the form for the client, so he can then hear life's themes.

DYNAMICS

In music, the parameter of intensity, or loud versus soft, is known as dynamics. A composer will often put dynamic indicators in the musical score as a means to guide the performer as to how loud or soft the music should be played. This is a very subjective aspect of performance of music. What one performer thinks as loud, another may think as not loud enough. The converse is true for playing quietly.

Dynamics play an important role in the expression of human emotions. How loudly one speaks or the intensity of the words is an aspect on which therapists concentrate in their evaluation of what is being said. When you think of how one verbally expresses anger, love, hate, compassion, you can imagine the dynamic contour of each expression. The congruence of dynamics and emotional expression is significant. When you think of normal expression of any of the above-mentioned emotions, you can also expect appropriate correlation to how loud or soft it is expressed. When incongruence is evident, there is an emotional component that is significant in the incongruence. That emotional component is what needs to be tapped into and explored musically with the client.

Speech has dynamics and melody working intricately together especially in the expression of emotion. These compliment each other to allow for a person's expression to be wide in variety. When a client is speaking in a subdued dynamic and a very monotone melodic contour, what might you conclude? Of course, you should always consider the content as well, but the way in which the content is portrayed is of utmost importance. Matching the client's melodic inflection as well as dynamic expression is often an excellent way of establishing a communication base. On an unconscious level, there is a feeling of being understood, a connection is made.

When involved in the physical playing of instruments, the energy or dynamic with which one engages in playing is of great significance. This energy is coming from an internal frame of reference. It is being channeled through the physical being, through an instrument, into audible sound. The instrument the client chooses, as well as how he plays the instrument, may be either conscious or unconscious; nevertheless, there is a purpose for the choice. Therefore, the audible sound becomes a portrait for the client of which he may or may not be aware. He acts upon the stimulus, gathers feedback, and alters his playing if needed. With this, a musical picture comes to life. The music therapist, with the understanding of the importance of musical expression, can utilize and work with this sound portrait.

Dynamics is one of the most important factors when concentrating on feeling states. The feeling state of the client seems to be most accurately portrayed and expressed through the dynamic level on which he plays. As stated earlier, when looking at the meaning of the words being spoken, you must consider the context in which the dynamic is played. As you consider context, you look for congruence between what is played, its dynamic, and the manner in which it is played.

Our daily life is filled with various forms of sounds and dynamics. The combination of life sounds can have many effects on people, both positive and negative. I often will do exercises with my clients regarding the awareness of dynamics in their life. Many come to see that at times there is too much "noise" at too loud a level. In this environment, their stress often increases. They speak of how to decrease the dynamic to increase focus, productiveness, as well as relaxation. Many also get in touch with the dynamic of their speaking voice and body language. They learn how these affect interpersonal relationships. Through these musical exercises, people find new ways of understanding their own process as well as their effect on those around them.

HARMONY

> *. . . music too, in so far that it uses audible sound, was bestowed upon us for the sake of harmony. And harmony, which has motions akin to the revolutions of the Soul within us, was given by the Muses to him who makes intelligent use of the arts, not as an aid to irrational pleasure, as is now supposed, but as an auxiliary to the inner revolution of the Soul, when it has lost its harmony, to assist in restoring it to order and concord with itself."*

—Plato

This statement makes a powerful suggestion not only as to the power of harmonic structure, but also to the concept of using music as therapy. When Plato speaks of "him who makes intelligent use of the arts," he is speaking to all creative arts therapists, but most importantly, to the music therapist.

Throughout history, harmony has undergone an evolution and has been taught in all college-level music programs. It begins with a relationship to mathematical correlations. It is the relationship of the natural frequency of a vibratory medium and its overtones. It can be broken down to basic elements of the root, intervals above the root, the building of chords, and then through harmonic progressions.

The harmony is the support for melody. Within harmony, there is an underlying principle of tension and resolution in music. Tension and resolution are also aspects of life. These can be related to feeling states and more explicitly, mood.

Harmony has the power to imitate as well as evoke mood. A client's affect can shift through listening to harmonic progressions. Because of the nature of harmonic structure, the client assimilates both the true physical and aesthetic nature of the combined notes and can be affected by them. As you look at life, the feeling states that you pass through might be placed on the tension-resolution continuum. Love and hate, for example, would be at opposite sides of the spectrum. Within the feeling states themselves, there may also be tension-resolution issues. In looking at love, for example, there are many variations of the tension-resolution principle.

Finding the harmony with oneself is often the goal in therapy. To feel that all is well within and have that feeling reflected in interactions with another is often what is searched for and needed. The principle of harmony is basic in everyday living. Understanding this and portraying it through music is very powerful.

RHYTHM

Rhythm is one of the most powerful overall tools the music therapist has to engage the client. Gaston (1968) writes:

> When the musics from all the cultures of the world
> are considered, it is the rhythm that stands out as
> most fundamental. *Rhythm is the organizer and the*

energizer. Without rhythm there would be no music, whereas there is much music that has neither melody or harmony. Combinations of rhythm, melody, harmony, and counterpoint have been in existence less than one thousand years, but rhythm has been the music of millions for many thousands of years. It is rhythm alone that makes possible the temporal order of music. For most people it is the rhythm that provides the energy of music, be it small or great. . . the unique potential of rhythm to energize and bring order will be seen as the most influential factor of music. (P. 17)

Robert Tussler (1991) also states the importance of rhythm, but more as it relates to our being both psychological and physiological. He says:

Of equal importance is the element of motion given form by rhythm. Our Being is in perceptual motion from conception to the moment the organism ceases to function. Music's flow is intertwined with man's rhythmic flow. Some insist that tones have a life of their own, which may be true, but there is no music without rhythm. It may be unmetered, such as Gregorian Chant, but that it no way indicates that its flow is not organized rhythmically. Changing rhythms and tempos are as much a part of our physiology and psyche as are the lifeblood of music. (P. 38)

Rhythm is a very important aspect of music, as well as life. In life, there are certain speeds by which things are done. Racing to get to work, and taking time for rest are just two examples of the relationship of rhythm and life.

The human body operates on the principle of rhythm in heartbeat, respiration, and brain waves. Mannerisms, gestures, and speech are all tied to rhythm. Being keenly aware of these relationships and noticing the rhythm indicators is very important. Observing and understanding these relationships provides a rhythmic base for communicating and establishing a musical or rhythmic bond. The bond, conscious on your part, is created almost subliminally for the client. It is much like empathy, where the client feels the connection, but is not sure why. This can be accomplished musically in various ways. Improvisation, matching pre-recorded music to the emotional or physical state, or by how you musically react to the client are but a few. Matching the voice rhythm of the client with yours, or his rhythmic movement in space, however small it might be, are some examples of responding to the client in a rhythmic sense. When working with a client, if you understand and get in touch with his rhythm, it is often an important step in getting him to trust you and the music. From this base, he can open up and explore new rhythms in their life.

TIMBRE

The quality of a sound is timbre. The timbre can often be thought of as the tone color of an instrument or voice. How is it that two violinists play the same musical passage identically, and one seems to be more to your liking? It might possibly be the timbre that makes the difference.

Some words that describe timbre are: warm, thin, thick, lush, cold. It is the "feeling" of the overall sound of an instrument that you are trying to describe, almost as if you were to describe its aura. In the same vein, we talk about people. Certain types of people just "feel" good to be around. They may be warm, generous, and giving. While others may be harsh, cold, and overbearing. Timbre is a necessary part of any instrument just as it is a necessary part of every personality. To understand one's timbre is to have a glimpse into one's soul.

SUMMARY

In looking at the various elements of music you can see that each one has its own unique relationship to life and the human condition. We notice that humankind's need to organize and to make sense of sounds has led us to develop scales, form, harmonic progressions, etc. When these various elements are combined, a musical composition may arise. When the composition arises, it represents some aspect of the person's psyche who composed it. The notes, form, rhythm, etc., came from both a conscious and unconscious level and therefore represent a significant musical picture of the person.

To the listener, the composition acts as a sound mirror. The listener reacts in some way to the sounds he perceives, and on that level the reaction becomes a mirror for a part of his internal frame of reference. This reaction can be at a conscious or unconscious level, and this can be explored in the music therapy session. Verbal descriptors of the music are often the descriptors of what he is going through, and a part of his psyche.

For example, an airline stewardess was in a session where the focus of the activity was on what images were immediately stimulated by the music. She had an instantaneous reaction to quick rhythms in a certain piece. She described the images as "fast and somehow shallow." This music also made her "uncomfortable," not only because of the image, but also because of the quickness. As she spoke, she continued relating how much she disliked this momentary musical experience. She went on to say her thoughts were "racing" that day and that she had to make some "quick" decisions regarding her living situation. As she spoke, her rate of speech increased, and she appeared more anxious. I helped her see the connection between the music and her current life situation. They were similar, and both very uncomfortable for her. She said she wished everything could just "slow down" and that she could feel "less pressured." I asked her to analyze her body sensations, the tension and her breathing pattern. From this point, I began improvising on the guitar. I had her focus on the music and to begin letting go of the body tension by breathing through the tension. I then gave the suggestion of letting her thoughts become slower with her breathing. As she calmed down, her body language appeared less defensive and tight, and her speech became less pressured. I then improvised one melodic line and had her focus on that line. I asked her to describe the line and what she was feeling as she listened. She spoke with clarity and focus as she described the monophonic melody. I invited her to think of only one aspect of her current life situation. She sat silently for a few moments and then began talking of her being afraid to make a change in her living situation. As she worked through the thought, I continued improvising, attempting to match her rhythm and vocal melodic inflections. Her affect changed. She looked contemplative, focused, and more in tune with one aspect of her thought process. The musical experience had allowed her to be more in touch with her physical and mental rhythm. She saw the connection between the music and her behavior, and, even more, she allowed the music to open a doorway to a different mode of cognitive functioning. In entering this mode of functioning, she was able to make a bit of progress in that very trying day.

Music is a gift. It can be entertaining, relaxing, energizing, sad, soulful, contemplative, and creative. Through all these things that **IT** is, for many **IT** becomes therapeutic. The special gift of music then, is that one can find his way through the music, with the aid of his guide, to a better place.

REFERENCES

Apel, W. (1972). *Harvard dictionary of music, 2nd ed.* Cambridge, MA: The Belknap Press of Harvard University Press.

Gaston, E.T. Ed. (1968). *Music in therapy.* New York: The Macmillan Co.

Tussler, R.L. (1991). *Music: catalyst for healing.* Alkmaar, Netherlands: Drukkerij Krijgsman.

Chapter 3

THE MUSIC THERAPY GROUP:
STRUCTURE AND TECHNIQUES

With three or more people there is something bold in the air: direct things get said which would frighten two people alone and conscious of each inch of their nearness to one another. To be three is to be in public, you feel safe.

-Elizabeth Bowen (1938)

VALUE OF GROUPS

Maslow has said "If ordinary [individual] therapy may be conceived of as a miniature ideal society of two, then group therapy may be seen as a miniature ideal society of ten . . . in addition we now have empirical data that indicate group therapy can do some things that individual psychotherapy cannot (1970, P. 263)." Carl Rogers (1968) feels that the group experience is a driving force for the exploration of oneself. The group experience helps alleviate loneliness, empowers the client to grow and to risk change.

In these statements there are two important premises. The first is that the group is a model for how people behave in society. Behaviors and relationships that clients engage in through the group process are those they also utilize in real life. The second premise is that because of the group process, and the relationships formulated throughout it, clients can make progress towards health if they so choose.

CRITERIA FOR THE EFFECTIVE GROUP

The group process affords for the client many possibilities for growth. Based on Yalom's work (1975), Magden and Shostrom (1974) developed a rating sheet for groups that looked at eight dimensions of group effectiveness. These dimensions can be observed as the group proceeds through various levels of operation. Growth of the group members could be evidenced as they engage in these various dimensions. The dimensions are:

1. *Catharsis*. Group members often ventilate feelings /or experiences.
2. *Group as a second family*. Group members identify the therapist and/or other members in family roles.
3. *Awareness*. Group members become more aware of their thoughts, feelings, and or bodily responses.
4. *Group cohesiveness*. Group members appear involved in the group.
5. *Receiving information*. Group members appear to be open to instructions, advice, and suggestions from the therapist.
6. *Imitative behavior*. Group members model their behavior after the therapist.
7. *Faith in the process*. Group members' behavior suggests that the group process will work for them.
8. *Giving and receiving help*. Group members appear to help one another through support and reassurance. (P. 322)

There are two additional dimensions, which Yalom (1975) lists, that are also important in the group process. They are

9. *Universality*. Group members appear to get insight into the "universal commonness" of their ideas, feelings, and behavior.
10. *Altruism*. Group members appear to feel a sense of caring or love for one another. (P. 322)

MUSIC THERAPY GROUPS

Music therapy in a group setting involves using music as the primary stimulus during the session to help the clients: (1) become aware, express, and explore feeling states; (2) gain insight into problem areas; (3) find resolutions and learn coping skills. These goals are accomplished through a wide variety of musical experiences. One of the reasons for this book is to give examples of these diverse activities.

Plach (1980) lists eight guidelines for planning and implementing music therapy for groups. They are as follows:

1. The chosen activity should be appropriately in tune with the individual symptomotology, individual and group needs, and within whatever conceptual, integrative, or physical limitations are existent within the group.
2. Music chosen for a session must take into consideration cultural and age factors existent within the group.
3. The amount of structure contained in the activity is contingent upon the level of functioning of the group and its individual members.
4. The level of participation of the leader in the music activity is determined by what the group needs in order to experience the activity to its fullest potential.
5. All individual and group responses to a music activity are valid responses.
6. Whenever appropriate, communicate immediate observations of behavior in the music activity to the group and/or individuals in the group.
7. Whenever appropriate, refer back to the initial activity and group or individual responses to the activity.
8. Whenever appropriate, explore within the group ways of integrating newfound insights, behaviors, or skills into situations outside of the group. (P. 12)

These are good guidelines for the music therapy group. The success of the group, however, is only partly determined by the preceding guidelines. The process through which the group goes also determines the success of the group. This process can be thought of as a dynamic action that flows from the moment the clients enter the room until they leave. The action is set up by that which they bring into the session and is completed with that which they remember after they leave the room. The therapist who possesses the qualities discussed previously and his overall therapeutic ability helps further this process.

STAGES OF THE MUSIC THERAPY SESSION

The music therapy session has three main stages: beginning, middle, and end. It seems that many inexperienced therapists get stuck in only concentrating on the middle stage, often forgetting or not noticing that two other stages are being left out. These other stages are very important, for they enable the cycle of the group to connect all that is before and all that is after, and thus cannot be ignored.

The Warm Up

The beginning of the session I call the warm up. It can also be called the set up because that is what you are really doing, setting up the session as you assess where each member is at emotionally/cognitively. This is a crucial point in deciding ultimately what plan, if any, you are going to use in the session. You should have at your fingertips many types of activities/interventions available and the ability to implement these into sessions quickly.

As the clients enter the room, I may or may not have music playing. If I do, it is usually instrumental. At times, it might be the music that ended the previous session, which can bring a sense of continuity. Whenever possible, I try to actually be playing (improvising) guitar, piano, or a melodic percussion instrument when they arrive. Live music has a wonderful way of welcoming clients, as you have the ability to immediately change what you are playing to acknowledge or greet clients as they arrive. After their arrival, I individually greet them and learn the names of new members. I feel it is important then to just talk for a few moments. This allows you to key into what they are bringing into the session as well as establishing rapport. Below is a list of topics I generally cover at the beginning of the warm up.

How they are doing (emotionally, physically).
What has been going on with them since the last session.
Whether they were able to apply anything they learned from
  the last session to daily life.

Any musical thoughts or experiences they might have had
since last session, for instance, have they heard a new song
they liked.

If appropriate I may employ a little humor such as a joke or ask
if any one has heard a good joke lately. (This is often a
wonderful way of breaking up any tension for new
members.)

The set up part of the warm up concludes with a transition into
talking about what the session will focus on that day. The focus is
determined by the goals the treatment team has set forth, as well as
by the general feeling that I am getting from the group at this time.
A brief synopsis of the type of activity is given. This will often
help alleviate any fears or apprehensions of new members of the
group. We then begin the musical portion of the session.

I usually have a time of focus on the sound of a quartz toning
bowl. The bowl is fourteen inches in diameter and one foot tall.
When stimulated by a rubber mallet, it produces the tone of "B." It
has a wide range of dynamic capability, so there is control of how
loud the note is actually produced. I invite group members to come
and put their hands in close proximity to the bowl in order to feel
the actual vibration. I also ask them to focus on their breathing—to
allow it to become longer and deeper. This exercise is very good
for helping clients become centered and preparing them for the
music session.

If the group will be involved in playing instruments, there is an
additional warm up time in which the group experiments and
warms up on the instruments. Each group differs at this stage,
since musical warm ups are dependent on the musical activity and
focus of the session.

The Middle

The middle section of the session transitions out of the
beginning. This is the body of the session structure where the
clients are involved mainly in the musical activity. One of the most
important principles for a music therapist to understand is that any
response that the clients may have to the music activity is a valid
response. Clients' responses can vary widely to a selection of

music, an improvisation, or a basic activity. This response is what the client offers to you as an indicator of where they are. What you may perceive as a powerful "negative" response to a piece of music is just as valuable, in a therapeutic sense, as a powerful "positive" response. Many young therapists take a negative reaction personally. They feel that the session is not "working," or, worse yet, they have an attitude such as "How can they possibly react this way! I don't see, feel, or hear it that way. No wonder they're in the hospital!" It is important to understand that what the group offers to you, is offered. Take what they give you, learn from it, and work with it.

Within the middle section, the group also progresses into self-disclosure issues. At this time, your role can become quite varied, depending on the group. You may be an active or passive facilitator. You may be helping to direct the questions of the group, or merely sitting back letting the group self-develop. The one thing you always are is observant. You should watch not only the interactions between the participants but also their response and interaction with the music on an individual basis. You need to be alert as to your own emotional reactions to the musical, verbal, and nonverbal material going on within the group. As you observe these events developing in the group, you may intervene to give feedback to the group or individual members. Chapter 4 introduces many of the techniques that I have found valuable for intervention.

The End

The conclusion of any session can often be the most difficult. It must not be too abrupt, since the clients may have been experiencing many different levels of emotion, and with these experiences there must be a sense of closure before the session ends. There should be a transition from the middle portion of the session in a tactful way. You may want to indicate at some point that the group needs to think about coming to an end. I often say, "We are coming near to the end of our session so. . ." or "It's almost time to close." These statements allow the group to prepare for its ending, and summary.

I conclude most of my music therapy sessions in a similar fashion. I ask each group member to share one final thought from that group. As you read through the vignettes in the following chapters, you will see how this final moment brings the group to a sense of conclusion. Within each conclusion, there is, however, a look to the future. As each member shares, they hold a Harmony Ball that is passed to them from another member. This ball is about three inches in diameter and has a chime-like sound. This final bit of music helps tie the whole event together. I have used this for many years, and it has been successful with many clients. It concludes the group with its own sense of acceptance and Presence.

REFERENCES

Brammer, L. M., & E. L. Shostrom, (1982). Therapeutic psychology: fundamentals of counseling and psychotherapy 4th ed. Englewood Cliffs, NJ: Prentice Hall.

Maslow, A. (1970). Motivation and personality 2nd ed. New York: Harper and Row.

Magden, S. and E. Shostrom (1974). Unpublished paper presented to the annual meeting of the American Psychological Association, New Orleans, LA. Found in L. M. Brammer, & E. L. Shostrom (1982). Therapeutic psychology: fundamentals of counseling and psychotherapy 4th ed. Englewood Cliffs, NJ: Prentice Hall.

Plach, T. (1980). The creative use of music in group therapy. Springfield, IL: Charles C. Thomas.

Rogers, C. R. (1968). Reflection of feelings. Person Centered Review, 2, 375–377.

Rogers, C. R. (1968). The increasing involvement of the psychologist in social problems. California State Psychologist, 9:29.

Rogers, C. R. (1980). A way of being. Boston, MA: Houghton Mifflin.

Yalom, I. (1975). The theory and practice of group psychotherapy. New York: Basic Books.

Chapter 4

THERAPEUTIC STRATEGIES

*At bottom, and just in the deepest and most important things, we are
unutterably alone, and for one person to be able to advise or even
help another, a lot must happen, a lot must go well, a whole
constellation of things must come right in order once to succeed.*

—Rainer Maria Rilke

In Chapter 1, I spoke of Presence, Intuition, Knowledge, and
Common Sense. Presence, Intuition, and Common Sense are often
learned through the experiences you live through. They may be
considered intangibles, which are difficult to teach in a typical
classroom setting. They can tie into one aspect of Knowledge,
namely the knowledge of self. Another aspect of Knowledge is
learning through more traditional methods—namely by a teacher
or through books. Knowledge of how to do things, or why things
work—this is different from the knowledge of self. Through the
experience of gaining Knowledge, Presence, Intuition, and
Common Sense can be enhanced.

In the above quote by Rilke, I focus on "a lot must happen, a
lot must go well, a whole constellation of things must come right
in order once to succeed." As the facilitator of many music therapy
sessions, I find much truth in this statement. At times things can
happen by chance, but more often I am aware of the interactions of
the group and the direction in which it is moving. The fact that I
am aware is founded in a knowledge base that has been enhanced
by a sense of Presence, Intuition, and Common Sense.

I previously stated that each session ideally has three sections:
a beginning, middle, and an end. Even though the middle stage of
the session activity is highly musical in nature, verbal processing
and interaction can certainly be a major component. The
verbalizations usually revolve around the stimulation and process
of the music intervention. You must know when and how to listen,
to intervene, to ask questions, give feedback, or simply be silent. If

you are engaged in a musical improvisation with the clients, you must know when to lead, follow, listen, and redirect.

The music brings to the surface many issues for the clients. As issues arise, you need to be prepared to act both musically and verbally. As clients talk about the music and their process with it, you should be aware of many facets of their behavior, so that you can understand what they are actually saying. The following are some methods of attending to their behavior. I have found these helpful in all types of music therapy sessions.

NONVERBAL MESSAGES

Listening to the nonverbal message of the client is an extremely important component of the message they are sending. Nonverbal messages can come from facial expressions, body language—both fine motor and gross motor—how they are dressed, and voice quality.

Nonverbal messages that come out when a client is playing an instrument can be quite dramatic. Notice how he holds, touches, and plays the instrument. Is his verbal description of the sound actually what he is playing? Do his sounds make sense in a musical way? If his sounds do not make sense to him, what does he need to be shown or to find so that the music will make sense for him. Once this is found, how does the process or the resolution relate to his life?

LISTENING AND UNDERSTANDING VERBAL MESSAGES

As the clients talk about the music, they are speaking about it from their internal frames of reference. When discussing lyrics, they are often projecting themselves into the song as a means of expression. As they do this, they are often caught in a struggle of what these words, written by someone else, actually mean to them. They often wonder why they are having such a strong reaction. This also holds true for non-lyric music and the effect it has on clients. The clients' words combined with their body language, tone of voice, voice inflection, rhythm, and affect are giving you information.

When the clients are speaking or trying to describe musically their reactions, you may become an interpreter for them. You can help them see that through strong descriptions of music, they are describing an aspect of who they are. This aspect is in resonance with the music or a particular lyrical theme. So as you listen to their words, remember the musical relationships to life. Utilize the understanding of these relationships with the clients to help them move forward in their treatment.

The first step in listening is not to respond, but to understand that which they are giving you. What are they trying to say? What is the theme of their statements? Are they filled with questions? What is their point of view? What is so important that they want to tell you? Rogers (1980) feels that you must be secure in yourself to be a good listener. This sense of security is needed because if you are actively listening, you may actually be experiencing what the client is experiencing, and you must have the ability to return comfortably to your own world.

Egan (1990) offers these questions to ask yourself on listening:

1. How well do I read the client's nonverbal behaviors and see how they modify what he or she is saying verbally?
2. How careful am I not to over interpret nonverbal behavior?
3. How intently do I listen to what the client is saying verbally, noticing the mix of experiences, behaviors, and feelings?
4. How effectively do I listen to the client's point of view, especially when I sense that this point of view needs to be challenged or transcended?
5. How easily do I tune into the core messages being conveyed by the client?
6. How effective am I at spotting themes in the client's story?
7. What distracts me from listening more carefully? What can I do to manage these distractions?
8. How effectively do I pick up cues indicating dissonance between reality and what the client is saying?
9. To what degree can I note the ways in which the client exaggerates, contradicts himself or herself, misinterprets reality, and holds things back without judging him or her and without interfering with the flow of dialogue?

10. How effectively do I listen to what is going on inside myself as I interact with clients? (P. 121)

Now, as you ask yourself these questions about the verbal messages that the client gives you and how you listen to them, think of an improvisation or a composition created by a client. Run through these questions again and think of them more in musical terms in order to focus listening. For example, let me rephrase some of the above to read as follows:

1. How well do I read the client's interaction with the instrument or music to modify what he is saying musically or verbally? In this, I am observing the manner in which the client is holding the instrument, what kind of relationship he is having with it. Is this consistent with the general mood of the overt behavior or his words? Is the relationship with the instrument or music an extension of his mood

2. How intently do I listen to what the client is saying musically, noticing the mix of experiences, behaviors and feelings? Am I perceiving the musical aspects of what he is saying? I listen to the various musical properties discussed earlier and attempt to understand the relationship of these to what the client has said he feels.

3. How easily do I tune in to the core messages as the client describes or plays the music? I listen for the expression of deeper issues that perhaps the client has not yet been able to verbalize.

4. How effective am I at spotting musical themes in the client's story or improvisation ? These themes may be melodic, rhythmic, or a combination of both. Once again, musical themes are often representations of life components, which include life themes, emotions, and behaviors.

5. How effectively do I pick up cues indicating musical dissonance between reality and what the client is saying or playing? I watch and listen for congruence between what is verbally said or done, and musical representation of it. If they are incongruent, what is the client really trying to convey or express?

6. How in tune am I with what the music is doing inside me as I interact with the client? I must be in touch with my own counter-transference and/or projections. I must understand that what the music is stimulating in me is not necessarily what is going on with my client.

In asking yourself these questions, you have guidelines of what to look and listen for from your client.

LISTENING TO THE SILENCE

In music, silence takes on many roles. It can be a point of rest or reflection. Or it can facilitate a great sense of tension and apprehension. The skillful composer understands these qualities of silence, and so should the music therapist. If one views the session as a musical composition, there are times in the composition when silence will be appropriate. For the young therapist, these times may be difficult to sit through or assimilate. The experienced therapist and composer realize that silence is not only needed, but also dynamic.

Silence can have many meanings during a session. The client has reached the end of an idea and may be wondering what to say next. It may be a signal that the client is experiencing some particularly painful feeling that he is not ready to verbalize, whereas consciously he may want to express the feeling desperately. This may be an appropriate time to have the client try to play on instruments what they are trying to say. In essence, the instrument becomes the client's voice, and afterwards you work together to find the words that match the music.

The silence might be "anticipatory" in nature, wherein the client pauses, expecting something from the counselor—some reassurance, information, or interpretation. And finally, the silence might be that the client is thinking over what he just said. In this case, interruption of the pause may be inappropriate, since it might destroy the client's train of thought (Brammer and Shostrom, 1982).

The problem for many therapists is whether to interrupt the silence or wait for the client to go on. I don't think that there is a rule for exactly what to do when silence occurs, but rather a time to ask this question, "What's going on here?" before breaking the silence yourself.

UNDERSTANDING THE FEELING

The bridge that stretches from listening to responding and/or probing is the bridge of empathy I have spoken of this previously in regard to being Present. As you probably have already noticed, the sense of Presence is a large part of the whole therapy process. It is fluid, in that it moves from stillness to action, and as it does the environment seems to change with it.

Empathy is a way of listening, responding, and being. In the group experience, you must understand not only where the group is at a given moment, but also where the members are as they progress through the larger group process. You must therefore be an integral part of each member, while moving moment to moment with many. In this movement, you must be ready to act, intervene, direct, redirect, focus, and help the group in its journey. You should be able to accurately perceive what is going on within the group dynamic. When you are accurately in tune with the group, you will know how and if to respond. You should be quite selective in responding when you do so.

Verbalizations of feelings are indicators. When a client is involved in a feeling, there should be congruence between affect and verbalization. When there is not, there is confusion within the client, and you should help him out of this confusion. In helping him to express and identify feelings, you need to give yourself time to think and respond appropriately. This can be accomplished by utilizing short phrases that provide for this opportunity Hepworth, and Smiths (1978) suggest using lead-in phrases such as:

> "Kind of feeling"
> "Sort of saying"
> "If I'm hearing you correctly"
> "To me it's almost like saying"
> "Kind of made (makes) you feel"
> "So you feel"
> "So, as you see it"
> "I'm not sure I'm with you, but"
> "I somehow sense that maybe you feel"
> "It seems to you" "Like right now"
> "As I hear it, you"
> "Your feeling now is that"

"I sense that you're feeling"
"Your message seems to be,"
"So your world is a place where you"

These lead-ins can help in verbal processing of material that the music elicits. As you are more in touch with what the inner world of the client is like, the easier it is for you to respond appropriately.

The exploration of feelings allows the client to enter in places he may have not been before. It is one thing to feel, it is another to talk about the experience of feeling. If one is in an improvisation session, it is also another thing to play or express the feeling nonverbally. The use of video tape and/or audio tape is important in improvisations. The creation becomes a musical piece of art, like that of a visual piece of art. It is derived from a feeling base and transformed into sound. The moment of creation (feeling) can be looked at and examined from many different perspectives. Through this investigation, the client will begin to gain insight. In groups, the insight and sharing of one member may resonate another member to also initiate progress in therapy.

As one moves through feelings to insight, clients have an ultimate choice. What are they to do with the information they have learned? For each person, this process takes a different amount of time. But in each music therapy session, I end with looking at what each person can take, learn, or remember from the group experience.

GROUP FEEDBACK

Feedback is a way of helping another person consider changing his or her behavior. It is communication with a person that gives that person information about how he affects others. Feedback, when properly given, is a way of giving help. It is a corrective mechanism for the individual who wants to learn how well his behavior matches his intentions (Saretsky, 1977).

As the group progresses, one of the things that it will ultimately do is give feedback for the participants. As the leader, you should try to structure the feedback of the group to be productive.

Saretsky (1977) says helpful feedback can have many different qualities.

One quality is that the feedback should be descriptive. This refers to the describing of one's own reaction to a statement, improvisation, or behavior. This leaves the client free to use the information, or not. In being descriptive, it should also then become specific rather than general. You may often need to point out the exact word(s) the client use that need to be addressed. Musically, you may need to point out the exact spot in their musical response that gives them the feedback they need.

The feedback must be usable, in that it is directed toward behavior that the receiver can do something about. Frustration is only increased when a person is reminded of some shortcomings over which he has no control. Since it must be usable for the receiver, the receiver should be requesting appropriate feedback— it is solicited rather than imposed.

It is well timed. In general, feedback is most useful when offered at the earliest opportunity after the given behavior (depending, of course, on the other person's readiness to hear it, the support available from others, etc.).

When feedback is given in a therapy group, both giver and receiver have an opportunity, with others in the group, to check the accuracy of the feedback. Is it the impression of one person, or is it shared by others? One must remember that we do not all evaluate the same events in the same way. The group is an excellent place to explore the accuracy of feedback.

A trusted, nonthreatening source helps make the feedback more palatable. When the therapist is congruent and Present for the client, this can be the groundwork for trust. Not only does this make the feedback more palatable, but it is also a necessary ingredient in the therapeutic process. If clients do not feel they can trust you or the group, they will not open up and share.

YOUR BODY LANGUAGE

I am quite aware of my body language and the messages my body is sending to the clients. As a client speaks to me, I try to maintain an open and relaxed body posture, keep good eye contact, and also be aware of what kind of messages my facial expressions might be sending. This sends a nonverbal message of openness to the client and can help the clients feel comfortable in sharing thoughts and feelings.

Your body is a source of communication, just as your client's body communicates signals to you. As you develop your skills, be in touch with messages that *your* body is sending *to you.* Are your muscles getting tense over a certain subject? Did you notice your affect change as the client revealed information that may have bothered you? You must learn not only to perceive and control your nonverbal messages, but also to understand what they are sending to the client. As stated earlier, your posture, affect, and tone of voice all contribute in some way to what clients perceive as your Presence and willingness to be there for them. This does not mean that you become overly concerned with your every movement. Rather, these are skills that become second nature as you grow as a therapist.

REFERENCES

Brammer, L. M., & E. L. Shostrom, (1982). Therapeutic psychology: fundamentals of counseling and psychotherapy 4th ed. Englewood Cliffs, NJ: Prentice Hall.

Egan, G. (1990). The skilled helper: A systematic approach to effective helping. Pacific Grove, CA: Brooks/Cole Publishing Company.

Gaston, E. T. Ed. (1968). Music in therapy. New York: The Macmillan Co.

Hammond, D. C., D. H. Hepworth & V. G. Smith (1978). Improving therapeutic communication. San Francisco CA: Jossey-Bass.

Martin, D. (1983). Counseling and therapy skills. Monterey, CA: Brooks/Cole Publishing Company.

Maslow, A. (1970). Motivation and personality 2nd ed. New York: Harper and Row.

Madden, S. & E. Shorts. Unpublished paper presented to annual meeting of American Psychological Association, New Orleans, 1974 found in L. M. Brammer, & E. L. Shostrom. Therapeutic psychology: fundamentals of counseling and psychotherapy, 4th ed. (1982).

Magden, S. and E. Shostrom (1974). Unpublished paper presented to the annual meeting of the American Psychological Association, New Orleans, LA. Found in L. M. Brammer & E. L Shostrom. (1982). Therapeutic psychology: fundamentals of counseling and psychotherapy 4th ed. Englewood Cliffs, NJ: Prentice Hall.

Meier, S. & S. Davis (1993). The elements of counseling. Pacific Grove, CA: Brooks/Cole Publishing Company.

Pascal, E. (1992). Jung to live by: a guide to the practical application of Jungian principles for everyday life. New York: Warner Books.

Plach, T. (1980). The creative use of music in group therapy. Springfield, IL: Charles C. Thomas.

Rogers, C. R. (1968). Reflection of feelings. Person Centered Review, 2, 375–377.

Rogers, C. R. (1968). The increasing involvement in of the psychologist in social problems. California State Psychologist, 9:29.

Rogers, C. R. (1980). A way of being. Boston, MA: Houghton Mifflin.

Saretsky, T. (1977). Active techniques and group psychotherapy. New York: Jason Aronson, Inc.

Yalom, I. (1975). The theory and practice of group psychotherapy. New York: Basic Books.

Chapter 5

STORIES, MYTHS, AND MUSIC

*. . . Whenever a fairy tale is told, it becomes night. No matter where
the dwelling, no matter the time, no matter the season, the telling of
tales causes a starry sky and a white moon to creep from the eaves
and hover over the heads of the listeners. Sometimes, by the end of
the tale, the chamber is filled with daybreak, and at other times a
shard is left behind, sometimes a ragged thread of a storm sky. And
whatever is left behind is bounty to work with, to use toward the
soul-making . . .*

—Clarissa Pinkola Estes, Ph.D.

I first heard the story of Khdir (pronounced Ka-deer) from
Grant Rudolph at the Western Regional Conference for Music
Therapy at California State University, Northridge, in 1986. I sat
fascinated as he played an ostinato pattern on a hand drum while
telling this age-old story. My fascination then turned to being
mesmerized, and I found myself chanting a little chorus with Grant
and the other participants. When the story concluded, there was
applause, and a discussion of the story. The more I thought about
it, the more drawn I became to this technique of telling stories with
music. I started to learn how to play a hand drum, developed some
patterns, and learned how to talk and play at the same time!

As I began to take a closer look at stories and myths, I realized
that I needed to understand them better, the symbolic meaning and
implications for therapy. I turned to the writings of C. G. Jung and
his philosophy of how stories and myths are related to the psyche.
From here, I began to understand why the story had such an effect
on me.

UNCONSCIOUS CONNECTIONS

*Our unconscious is like a vast subterranean factory with intricate
machinery that is never idle, where work goes on day and night from
the time we are born till the moment of our death.*

—Milton R. Pirstein

Kaufman (1995) summarizes a basic tenet in Jung's
psychotherapy as being a creative and symbolic approach seeking
balance between conscious and unconscious forces. In discovering
this balance, the individual gains a fuller awareness to the meaning
of life.

Jung defines two levels of unconscious. One level is defined as
the Personal Unconscious. This is composed of elements that had
once been conscious and are easily retrievable. Jung says that it is
. . . the gathering place of forgotten and repressed contents, and has
a functional significance thanks only to these" (Jung, 1954, P.3).
He states further, ". . . this personal unconscious rests upon a
deeper layer, which does not derive from personal experience and
is not a personal acquisition but is inborn. This deeper layer I call
the *collective unconscious.*" Corsini (1984) defines the Collective
Unconscious as "universally inherited predispositions for psychic
functioning." (P. 591) Gerald Corey (1977) says, "This is the
storehouse of buried memories inherited from the ancestral past.
The collective unconscious contains the wisdom of the ages and
serves as a guide for human development." (P. 18) Jung (1954)
describes it as part of the psyche not being specifically individual,
but universal, which is in contrast to the personal psyche. Jung
feels that it contains contents and modes of behaviour that are
more or less the same everywhere and in all individuals.

In his Tavistock 2nd lecture (England, 1935), he describes it as
follows:

> The brain is born with a finished structure, it will
> work in a modern way, but this brain has its history.
> It has been built up in the course of millions of
> years and represents a history of which it is the
> result. Naturally it carries with it the traces of that

history, exactly like the body, and if you grope down into the basic structure of the mind you will naturally find the traces of the archaic mind. The deepest we can reach in our exploration of the unconscious mind is the layer where man is no longer a distinct individual, but where his mind widens out and merges into the mind of mankind— not the conscious mind, but the unconscious mind of mankind, where we are all the same. (P. 41)

Within the Collective Unconscious, there lie the Archetypes. This is the name to which Jung gives as those inherited thought forms and feelings that we all have in common. Kaufmann (1984) defines the archetype as "Primordial [from the beginning] concepts or visions embedded in the Collective Unconscious that correspond to conscious experience and are expressed symbolically through eternal themes in mythology, folklore and art. It is a universal thought form or idea that contained a large amount of emotion." (P. 121) Jung (1954) calls it "a typos [imprint], a definite grouping of archaic character containing, in form as well as meaning, mythological motifs." (P. 4)

Some archetypes that are common and come up in stories and myths are:

Persona: This is one of adaptation, it helps us in figuring out how to act in given situations. Ideally it is flexible, helps us in the roles we play. It is sometimes referred to as the actors' mask we wear.

Shadow: This is one of Jung's most important archetypes. It represents that aspect of us that we would not like to be. It is all those things that we would never recognize in ourselves and qualities we don't like in others. Because we can't recognize the attributes of the shadow within ourselves it is most experienced by a projection on to others.

Anima: That aspect of man that relates to the feminine Yin (Yin Yang) principle. This accounts for man's capacity for being emotional, expressing feelings, being able to relate in a personal way to others, being creative and spontaneous.

Animus: The Yang or masculine aspect that exists in women. The woman's animus helps in giving her strength, having the ability to be judgmental, and to be aggressive when necessary.

Self: The expression of an innate predisposition to experience meaning in life. The Self truly becomes known when we are faced with problems that bring us to a place of having to recognize and surrender to a higher authority, thus transcending the ego.

Hero: The channel of the greater than. He must be able to endure great pain to be transformed. When people are in a great struggle in their emotional growth, they will often call upon this archetype. When called upon, there are three stages that are engaged: departure, struggle, and return. When the struggle is over, the person returns with a more developed integration of who he is.

Old Man: That which brings us knowledge, reflection, insight, wisdom, cleverness, and intuition.

Mother: Maternal solicitude and sympathy, magic authority of the female, the wisdom and special exaltation that transcends reason. Any helpful instinct or impulse that cherishes or fosters growth and fertility.

The concept of the archetype revealing itself symbolically is most important in the Jungian approach. These symbols are the means by which the unconscious speaks or makes itself known. In order to find balance between conscious and unconscious, it is necessary to have access to the unconscious. According to Jung, one of the best ways to be in touch with unconscious elements is through dreams. Dreams contain archetypal material that can help clients in finding their way through the therapeutic process. Yet dreamwork is not the only method by which the unconscious becomes revealed. A large part of the symbolic revelation can also be accomplished through stories and myths. Consider the following quote by Jung regarding this important point: "In myths and fairytales, as in dreams, the psyche tells its own story, and the interplay of the archetypes is revealed in its natural setting" (Jung, 1948).

Stories have a unique role in most human lives. As children, they entertain, excite, calm, and teach us. The bedtime story is usually told with a backdrop of a dimly lit room with the words of wisdom that are often the last thing a child hears before drifting off to the land of dreams.

Stories seem to have a way of working things out. The characters often seem to have to overcome seemingly insurmountable obstacles. They are most often human or humanlike and go through incredible trials and tribulations. We come to care for the ones in danger or treated unfairly, and also despise those that cause suffering. Children want to hear about these characters and the story over and over again—as if the character and the story are also growing inside them, as a part of who they are becoming. Stories in this role aid in the psychological growth of a child. They offer lessons. Some are simple, and some are profound. They teach about what is right and wrong, what is good and bad, and often about what path to take or not.

I have found that as stories are being told, certain aspects of the story resonate with the listener. I feel that unconscious elements and/or archetypes are often seeking expression and are letting the listener know of this by being resonant with archetypal aspects of the story. Knowing this, it is then possible to investigate what needs expression.

MUSIC—THE ACTIVATING AGENT

As I absorbed these concepts and read more about the relationship of symbols, archetypes, and myth, I found the story of Khdir in the writings of Jung. Not only did he tell the story, he explained its symbolic nature in relationship to the psyche. I discovered that my interpretation was very similar to his! All my reading and research were beginning to pay off.

With each story I learned, its symbolic nature became evident. Even more, as I used the myth in the clinical setting, I observed its profound effect on my clients. They interpreted the morals of the story as well, at times gaining insight to the significance of the its relationship to their own psyche. Through this process, they were able to integrate the story and their involvement with it into their treatment. They would often take the information back to their primary therapist who would continue the work started in the music therapy session.

When I tell a story, music plays a large role in the telling process. Music has three basic roles: creating the setting for the story; as an aid in the telling of the story; and for the client to use as a vehicle of expression.

Creating the atmosphere

The music can set an atmosphere that opens a doorway for the client to experience the session. The rhythm of the music combined with the telling of the story can be a powerful method of creating mood. Rudolph (1988) states that the repetition of rhythmic motifs has the ability to produce an altered state, mainly because of the sense of boredom that settles in the listener. Through this boredom, the attention can shift elsewhere, yet it is still involved, on a subconscious level, with the rhythm. Sandner (1979) states that in a Navaho ceremony "monotony itself, by lowering the threshold of consciousness, allows the constantly repeated images to register on deeper subconscious layers." (P. 62) I feel that the attention is allowed to shift away from the rhythm, yet the perseverance of the rhythmic integrity engages and entrains the listener. This concept of entrainment is a "process in physics whereby two objects vibrating at similar frequencies will tend to cause sympathetic resonance" (Maranto, 1993, P. 159). A good example of entrainment is when you go to the beach and begin to feel that you are becoming part of the rhythm of the waves. You have a different physical sense of being, you are entrained with the ocean. In the same fashion, the listener moves into a different state of being through the rhythm you play. As the story is being told, clients can focus on the story while being in this quasi-altered state that is set up by the rhythm. Being in this state also allows for the story to resonate with archetypal unconscious—much like a dream.

The physical environment in which one tells the story is also important. I have found that when people are allowed to sit, or lie in a circle on large pillows, it is conducive to the listening process. Even if they are playing on instruments in parts of the story, I prefer to have them sitting on large pillows on the floor. This change in their physical position is one way to let them know that they are going to experience something different from their regular group therapy time.

Avoiding fluorescent lighting is preferred. I use as much natural light in the room as possible, and if more is needed I utilize regular lights with shades. I do not, however, use a large amount of light. I think that a subdued hue in the room is good and allows for, again, the sense that something different is going to happen in this hour.

Telling the story

Voice tone and pacing of the story can be learned and practiced. The voice should have a sense of center. It should be clear and resonant. There should be inflection and direction in the line, as if one were playing a melody with the voice. This should not be, however, to the point of exaggeration, which becomes distracting. The pacing of the words and sentences is improvisatory in nature. The pacing comes from understanding the story in its entirety. By understanding, I do not mean just the "moral of the story is . . ." but rather a true knowledge of all its facets and their relationship to the psyche. Along with this is how it relates to you personally. When you can understand the story and its relationship to your own life, then you can feel the significance of the words leading to phrases and sentences on a much more intuitive level. On this level, as you tell the story, you become the story. As musicians, this is similar to the feeling derived as you play a piece of music. It no longer becomes an object outside of you, but it becomes part of who you are. The performance of the piece becomes a significant expression of your own soul. This is how it is for me and a story I tell as well as the music I play. The clients can feel this connection from me, and therefore it becomes a bridge to them. The story, the music, the pacing, and the voice tone become a new entraining and enlightening experience to the client group, one that they usually never forget.

Vehicle for expression

In many of the stories I tell, the clients have an opportunity to play as part of the story or as a response to it. If they are playing as part of the story, it is during a time when there is a musical interlude and I am not actively engaged in the verbal telling of the story. If I am asking them to respond to the story musically, it is usually after the story has finished and may come before or after a time of verbal processing of the meaning of the story. The clients have the opportunity to express the impact of the story. I have found that through this expression the clients are drawing from the energy of pure emotion to make musical sounds. These are offered as a means to communicate what is often hard to communicate, and the whole process can truly be cathartic.

Music holds the entire experience together. This is accomplished through attributes of music such as timbre and melody of voice, form of the story, harmonic movement of accompaniment, and overall rhythm of not only the story, but the entire experience. The intervention takes on a quality unlike a typical verbal processing group; it opens doorways for the clients to enter, and by entering they discover more of who they are.

REFERENCES

Ackroyd, E. (1993). *A dictionary of dream symbols*. London: Blandford.

Corey, G. (1977). *Theory and practice of counseling and psychotherapy*. Monterey, CA: Brooks/Cole Publishing Co.

Corsini, R., & D. Wedding (Eds.) (1984). *Current psychotherapies*. 3rd Edition. Itasca, Ill.: F. E. Peacock Publishers, Inc.

Corsini, R., & D. Wedding (Eds.) (1995). *Current psychotherapies*. 5th Edition. Itasca, Ill.: F. E. Peacock Publishers, Inc.

Estes, C. (1995). *Women who run with the wolves: myths and stories of the wild woman archetype*. New York: Ballantine Books.

Estes, C. (1995). *Theater of the imagination*. Vols. 1 & 2. Boulder: Sounds True Audio.

Jung, C. G. (1935). *Archetypes of the collective unconscious*. In F, pp.52–95 of *The collected works of C. G. Jung*. Princeton, NJ: Princeton University Press.

Jung, C. G. (1964). *The collected works of C. G. Jung*. Princeton, NJ: Princeton University Press

Jung, C. G. (1964). *Man and his symbols*. London: Aldus Books.

Kaufmann, Y. (1985). *Analytical Psychotherapy* found in *Current Psychotherapies*. 5th Ed. by R. J. Corsini. Monterey, CA: Brooks/Cole Publishing Company.

Hall, J. (1983). *Jungian dream interpretation*. Toronto: Inner City Books.

Heal, M. & T. Wigram (1993). *Music therapy in health and education*. London: Jessica Kingsley Publishers, Ltd.

Hunt, M. trans. (1948). *Grimm's fairy tales*. London Routledge and Kegan Paul.

Maranto, C. D. (1993). *Applications of music and medicine* in M. Heal & T. Wigram (1993). *Music therapy in health and education*. London: Jessica Kingsley Publishers, Ltd.

McAdams, D. P. (1993). Stories we live by: personal myths and the making of the self. New York: William Morrow and Co.

Pascal, E. (1992). *Jung to live by: a guide to the practical application of Jungian principles for everyday life*. New York: Warner Books.

Rudolph, G. (1988). *Dreamsinging; sounding the depths of psychic images*. Unpublished Masters Thesis, Human Relations Institute.

Sandner, D. (1979). *Navaho symbols of healing*. New York: Harcourt, Brace, Jovanovich.

Simonson, H. P. (1971). *Strategies in criticism*. New York: Holt, Rinehart and Winston.

Stein, M. & L. Corbett (Eds.). (1992). *Psyche's stories: modern Jungian interpretations of fairy tales*. Vol. 2. Wilmette, IL.: Chiron Publications.

Von Franz, Marie-Louise. (1970). *Interpretation of fairy tales*. NY: Spring Publications.

Chapter 6

GROUP VIGNETTE:
STORIES, MYTHS, AND MUSIC

Myths incorporate archetypal symbols that remain viable today if our imaginations are active enough to make us conscious of and curious about, our origins and our destiny.

-H. P. Simonson

CLINCAL SETTTNG

The clients involved in this vignette are all part of a chemical dependency twelve-step recovery program. The clients are living in an unlocked group environment. They are involved in various lectures and groups throughout the day Music therapy is held in a separate building, and a staff member escorts the clients to the session. The clients that are part of this group are at various levels in their recovery.

THE CLIENTS

Michael - A 28-year-old white man who is depressed and an alcoholic. His father died approximately two months prior to hospitalization. He has some unresolved feelings regarding the death of his father and is also dealing with his alcoholism. He has been in the hospital for 6 days.

Vivian - A 39-year-old white woman who has had multiple admissions for depression to psychiatric hospitals. She has been drinking excessively and has blacked out on several occasions. She has been involved in three failed marriages. From the age of 9 to 14, her father and her older brother sexually and emotionally abused her. She has also been diagnosed with Post Traumatic Stress Disorder and has been in the hospital for 14 days.

James—A 45-year-old black man who has several children. He is depressed and an alcoholic who grew up with no father in the home and several siblings. He has had a difficult time holding a job. He has been in the hospital for 18 days.

Kathy—A 32-year-old white woman who was emotionally abused by her mother. Her husband, who is currently in the military, is verbally abusive to her. She is the mother of two children. Prior to admission, she tried to commit suicide by overdosing on antidepressants. She is depressed and has been in the hospital for 10 days.

Mark—A 22-year-old white cocaine addict. He has recently lost his job. He is guarded and not really investing in the group process. He has been a poor historian regarding his past and feels that he doesn't have a problem. He has been in the hospital for 4 days.

Bill—A white 33-year-old alcoholic. He is also been quite guarded in groups not sharing much during his treatment. He is professional who played a great deal of percussion in high school. He has been in the hospital 10 days.

THE SETUP

When I tell the story of Khdir, I have the group participate in the story musically through an improvisation. I therefore plan as to the instrumentation that I would like utilized, and so the instruments for the group are pre-chosen before the group arrives. The instruments are laid out on the floor in a circle. In the center of the circle is a 14-inch 100% quartz toning bowl that produces a resonant pitch of "B" when played. Around the instruments are large pillows on which to sit. For the following group session, the instruments that were used were: two slit drums, one with three bass slits, the other a soprano with five slits; two paddle drums; one wood block; and one cabasa. I play a 12-inch hand drum for the warm up and the telling of the story.

As the group entered the room, I had Ray Lynch's "Only an Enjoyment" from Nothing Above My Shoulders But The Evening playing in the background. This is a piece that creates nice atmosphere for the clients when they walk into the room. I have found that when trying to find music such as this for the beginning or ending of groups there are two ways to find out if it is truly effective for the purpose for which it is intended. One is to try to place yourself in your clients' shoes and then physically walk into the room and experience the music as you might think they might experience it as they enter. Does it affect you the way you thought it would? How does the music match the atmosphere you have created for this group today? Is this music a true prelude to the group that will help them enter into the music therapy session? The other way to find out the effectiveness of a piece is simply to ask the clients. Ask questions such as, "What do think of this music that is playing?" or "As you enter and hear this music, what kind of sensations are going through your body?" "How does it make you feel?" The clients will usually tell you exactly what they are experiencing. From their responses you can make decisions about your entering music. You can also compare what you felt as you walked into the room to what they say they are feeling or experiencing

The lighting was a mixture of natural sunlight and one lamp. As it was nearing sunset, the natural light was growing dim. This combined with the one lamp made for a very nice atmosphere.

THE SESSION

Beginning-Warm Up

As the group entered, I greeted each one of them by name and invited them to sit in front of the instruments on the floor. I decreased the volume on the CD player. I had worked with all these clients before so there were no new clients to introduce to the concept of music therapy. As they settled, I asked them how the day was going for them. This is an open-ended question, which allows the clients to disclose to you whatever they might want to share at that moment. From this information I can quickly assess the appropriateness of the group I have planned.

Ron   So . . . How are things today? (About 10 seconds pass, as the group looks at one another.)

Michael Well, I'm having a tough day . . . in group I started thinking about my father, our relationship . . . or lack of one. I'm not sure what is really going on with that.

Vivian   I'm feeling . . . I guess kind of sad. I'm trying to deal with all that stuff from when I was a kid. That's all.

James   Well I'm feeling better today, up ya know. I know that I am going to stay sober, get with the program, get my wife and family back. So I feel good today.

Kathy   I'm confused. I guess I'm starting to see things about my marriage, my husband. I'm unhappy with how things have been going, but I don't know what to do about them.

Mark   I'm OK today. Nothing new.

Bill   Me too, nothing really new to report.

As each one of them replies, I focus on them. I give them affirmative body gestures, such as nodding my head and at times leaning slightly toward them. Interspersed are a few verbal acknowledgments such as, "Uh huh" or an affirmative "Mm Hmm." Mark appears a bit less guarded in body language today, yet it seems that with his response he almost wants to say more, but declines. Bill, with his short response is looking at the instruments and a bit fidgety. He is in front of the 5 tone slit drum. He reaches for the mallets and begins to play.

Bill   I use to play a lot of percussion in high school. (Bill plays a pleasant melodic two-measure phrase. He then begins to repeat it over and over again.)

I let this continue just to see where it leads. I don't want to discourage immediate playing unless it gets out of hand. This exploration can serve as a model for others, and it also might be initially tapping into a part of the child that is in everyone.

Vivian   Are we going to have to play today?

When a member starts with a defensive posture, I try to minimize the threatening aspect of the group and show that if they try, something good may come out of it.

Ron	We're going to be playing a little today . . . I think you'll find that this group will be a bit different from ones you've had in the past. I have found that many people have a good bit of fun in this group as well as getting some things out of it. (The group was then attending to Bill as he played. He played for about a minute and looked up at the group.)
Bill	This is cool. (He began to reach for the paddle drum in front of Kathy.)

Bill seems to have a bit of nervous energy and a problem with boundaries as he reaches for another member's instrument. I feel the need to keep the group focused as a whole and therefore need to get Bill out of the playing of instruments now that he has already explored one.

Ron	That was really good playing, but before we start with the instruments why don't we begin the group with the toning bowl, get centered, and then we'll talk about what we're going to do with the instruments today. (Bill complied with this request and put down the mallets from the slit drum.) As you hear the tone from the bowl, take a few deep breaths, and if you are comfortable with closing your eyes, allow them to close and let your attention move to your breathing and the sound that you hear. (I begin the eliciting the sound from the bowl by rubbing a rubber mallet around the outside edge.) Just breathe deeply and slowly and let the sound come into you.

As this is being done, the clients appear to become physically more relaxed. Body tensions seem to change as well as affect. I do this for about two minutes at a moderate volume level. I like beginning with this activity, especially for new group members, as it means right from the start that this is going to be a different experience from that of their group therapy. I believe that the mind becomes more focused and attention is heightened in a relaxed way to allow for a music experience.

Ron   As the sound gets quieter and fades away, open your
       eyes. (Each member of the group opens their eyes).
       Everyone OK? Good. Let me tell you a bit about what we
       are going to do today. First, we are going to do a bit of
       playing. Then, I am going to tell you a very old tale, a
       tale about two people, one named Khdir, and the other
       named Moses. After the tale, we're going to talk about it.
       And that's about it, that's what we're going to be doing
       today.

With this introduction, I give them enough information about the group so that they have an idea as to what is going to happen.

Vivian   But I can't play music . . . I've never been able to play.

Again Vivian is defensive and perhaps a bit threatened. Instead of confronting this fear, I decide to try to coax her into being more amenable to the idea of playing and move ahead with the group.

Ron   Well let's just give it a try and see what happens. If
       everyone could take the instrument that is in front of
       them and just explore it for a few minutes. Try to find all
       the different sounds that you can make with it.

Mark is having a little trouble figuring out the cabasa, so I show him the proper way to play it, as well as inviting him to explore other ways to play. Bill is again playing the pattern that he was playing earlier. The other members of the group are tentatively playing their instruments. Michael has the three tone slit drum; Vivian the wood block; James and Kathy each have a paddle drum; Mark the cabasa; and Bill has the five tone slit drum. Vivian is not doing much with the woodblock, she appears uninterested in this warm-up. The other members are all looking as though they are getting involved with this activity. As with most warm ups and exploration of instruments, the sound from the group is chaotic.

Ron   OK, let's focus back here to me. Thanks. Any questions regarding your instruments? Is everyone OK with the instrument they have been playing?

I usually offer this second question to allow anyone to change, as I do have other instruments in the background.

Ron   Let's explore for a few minutes on how we can all play together. How to sound like a group.

Mark   Yeah, right (sarcastically).

Vivian I don't think that is possible.

Vivian continues with her negative expressions toward the playing of the instruments. When this occurs, it is easy to be distracted. I keep focused, as the group needs to move forward

Ron   Well, let's just see. The first thing we need to understand is that there has to be something basic that keeps us all together, and that is what we call the beat. So, just to get us all together, I would like for you to just imitate what I am playing. (I then demonstrate a steady beat at about 60 beats per minute, with no accents. The members join in one by one.) Great, now let's organize that beat by accenting the first one of four so that it sounds like this ....1, 2, 3, 4, etc. (The group follows.) Let's do two more sets of 4 then stop when we get back to one. Great! OK, now if we continue to just do that we will all stay together, but it could get a bit boring. So what you now can experiment with is playing around the beat. Let me and Bill demonstrate for you, OK Bill?

I pick Bill because I have confidence in his playing as being a model for others. He has an understanding of playing with the beat as well as around the beat. Many times, I take time out with each member of the group to play one on one with me to find some sense of security of playing with a beat. Today I did not do that as I could tell already by their brief exploration that they could probably all fit into a beat, even Vivian.

Bill	Sure.
Ron	OK. I'll keep the beat, and Bill will play around the beat, or you can think of playing sounds between the beat also. (We demonstrate.)
Mark	Cool.
Kathy	Can we just listen to you guys play?
Ron	Not today, we're all going to play. So let's all try it together. First of all just match my beat. Then, as you feel more comfortable, play around with it in whatever way you like. If you think you are lost, just come back to the beat with me. OK, everyone start with me.

The group starts with me, and then an improvisation develops. Michael, on a slit drum, initially did not want to move away from the beat, but he then started with some simple eighth note patterns between the beats. His tentative movement away from the beat fits in with his fear of not doing things correctly, or "as he was told." Vivian never really strayed from the beat at all; she just kept the beat yet did not accent the first beat of a measure. She would just keep the same intensity with each strike of the woodblock. With the playing of this same beat over and over she found security, yet lacked the expression of accent. James got into exploring right away. His affect changed, and he was smiling and appeared to really be having fun. His mood seemed to match his playing well. Kathy also kept a simple beat on the paddle drum, much like Vivian. She did manage a few eighth notes here and there along with some first beat accents. Mark appeared to be enjoying the cabasa. He was exploring with all types of rhythmic patterns. He seemed to really get into his own instrument, and his body language became a bit more closed as he sort of hunched over the cabasa. This is actually typical of Mark, self-absorbed, appearing to interact with others musically as he was in the beat with them, yet physically and emotionally detached. Bill looked intense on exploring patterns on his slit drum. He seemed to be making sure that he fit into the beat and group well with his playing. This improvisation continues for about five minutes, and as it continued, the group began to bond more in a rhythmic coherence that was absent earlier. This approach to improvisation is quite directive and structured by me. I do this because the improvisation is to add to the involvement of the client in the story, and not so much to investigate self. What I have found is that by contributing to the story the group feels more part of the story and as secondary gain, they also bond together more as a group.

Ron   (As the playing continues) You all sound great! This is what we'll call "walking music" and will be part of the next section of this group. Let's bring this to a close like we did earlier. Everyone come back to this beat and then we'll do two more rounds of 4 beats and end on one. OK ... everyone's back now so ... 1, 2, 3, 4, last one, 1, 2, 3, 4, and 1. That was great!

Michael We actually sounded pretty good.

Mark   Sign us up! James, you were really goin' after it for a while there.

James   What can I say ... when you've got it, ... you've got it.

Kathy   That was fun, I can't believe I stayed with you guys.

Bill   You did great Kathy ... and so did you Vivian.

Vivian Yeah, like I really knew what was going on (in a sarcastic tone).

Knowing that Vivian has been having trouble with this group from the start, I decide to give her some positive attention for her role.

Ron   Actually, Vivian, you provided something really important for the group. Do you know what that was?

Vivian No.

Ron   Does anyone know what Vivian gave to the group that was so important?

Bill   She kept a real steady beat, even when you kind of played around with the beat, she was always really steady.

Ron   That's right. Did you know that, Viv?

Vivian Not really, I just felt comfortable with that, and it was easy.

Now if this was a group just focusing on improvisations, the dynamics of this group was already beginning to be evident, especially with Vivian. My next question to her may have been something like this: "If you could ask yourself this question, 'What feeling am I comfortable with, that is easy and steady?' What feeling would that be?" After identifying this feeling I might even ask Vivian to play it again now thinking about that feeling. But since the focus of the current group is to be the story and the responses to the story, I decided not to pursue this aspect of the improvisation.

Ron   Well, it was an important part of the group because it kept many people on task while they were playing. You provided a sense of a home beat that allowed people to go away from the home and return. So . . . that was what we will call "walking music" because as I tell the story there will be three times during the story that I will say, "And so, they walked on." When I say that, we will all play the walking music. Please put your instruments down for a few minutes and take a look at this hand drum that I am holding. Let me tell you a little bit about the different ways to play this drum and its relationship to the story you are about to hear. There are four basic ways that I will play the drum, and each way corresponds to something in life. The first way is the sound of your feet against the ground and it sounds like this (I play the center of the drum with a flat hand against the head). This is what our feet sound like as we walk upon the Earth. A second way of playing it is like *this* (rim shot of the index finger against the rim of the drum). This is the sound of sparks from a fire. Imagine the spark rising up from a fire. The third way of playing is like this (finger tips and/or nails brushing on the head of the drum, moving in a circular motion) . . . this is the wind. And the fourth way is the depth of the pond and it sounds like this (the thumb bounces off of the center of the drum). I am going to pass the drum around the circle, and I would like each one of you to try these four ways of playing this drum.

(The drum is passed around the circle and each member tries the four ways of playing it. As they do this I review the name of each technique with them and have them repeat the name after me.)

Ron   OK. You all seem to have a good grasp on how to play this. Later in the group, you will have the opportunity to play this drum again. Before the story starts, let's pick up the instruments and briefly review the rhythm that we will use for the "walking music." Throughout the story, I will be playing this rhythm (*I demonstrate a 4/4 beat that starts with a rim shot [beat one] then a flat hand against the head [beat two] and then a circular motion of the brushing wind sound [beats three and four]*). The cycle then repeats. I will then, at some point say, "And they walked on," which will signal all of us to play together our walking music. We will continue with the walking music until you see me go back to this story pattern. So let's try all of this together (we practice the sequence). Great . . . OK ready for the story? (We all stop playing.)

Up to this point of the group, I consider everything warm up for the actual story and processing of the story. The middle of the group now begins with the telling of the story.

The Middle

The following is how I tell the story. This is somewhat word for word, but remember that each story can be slightly different, depending on the group and how I am approaching it that day. The story also moves in its own flow, its own sense of rhythm. I can't indicate the pauses or flow of the sentence structure. It just moves, gradually and effortlessly. I actually begin not with the story, but with reviewing the four ways of playing the hand drum. As you will see, these four ways now take on a different meaning and lead into the story. The narrative begins with talking about the basic ways in which we listen or hear in this world.

Ron   There are four ways in which we hear in this world. Some of us hear through our feet, and it sounds like this (flat hand against the drum head, this is repeated in a steady rhythm as I talk). We hear from the sounds of our feet traveling across the earth. Some of us hear through the sparks in the fire (repeated rhythmic rim shot). And as the sparks float into the night sky we, listen . . . and hear. Some of us hear though the sounds in the wind (repeated circular movement of fingertips over the drumhead). We hear things that travel to us in the wind. Each one of us comes into this world knowing one way best how to hear. Yet we all search for the fourth way, which comes up from the depth of the pond, and it sounds like this (repeated beat of the thumb against the middle of the drumhead). When we put them all together, they sound like this

(I demonstrate a 4/4 rhythmic pattern integrating the 4 ways that also approximates the rhythm of the "walking music" developed earlier.)

Ron   And that will bring us to story time . . .

(I switch the pattern to the ostinato 4/4 beat I demonstrated earlier in the group, rim shot, flat hand, wind. This continues all the time I am talking until when I note that I stop playing.)

Ron   Once upon a time, long ago, or maybe not so long ago, there walked upon the Earth a man named Khdir. Khdir was that aspect of man that is sometimes thought of as God within himself. That part of man that is his own Self. And he was walking upon the Earth. As he was walking, he happened to run into Moses. Now, you all know who Moses was, right? He was the leader of the people. Now, Moses was walking along the road having his own difficult day when he met up with Khdir. Upon meeting Khdir, he says "Khdir, I see that we are traveling on the same path, perhaps we can walk this road together?" Khdir replies, "I don't know Moses, I will do things that you will probably not understand, and you will question me." And Moses says "No, I won't question you Khdir, I

promise." Khdir reluctantly agrees. And so . . . they
walked on.

(I indicate that this is where we are all to play together. The group
slowly joins in. I then return to the ostinato pattern. The group
fades out the walking music.)

Ron   It was morning as they began their journey. They walked
awhile until they came over a little hill. Below them, was
a small fishing village. In this fishing village, each family
had its own fishing boat that was anchored in the harbor.
The people of this village made their living from the fish
they caught. Not only was it the chief means of income, it
was also their main source of food. Khdir jumped into the
water and with a small bit he drilled a small hole in each
one of the boats. This caused each boat to sink.

(My ostinato stops.)

Ron   Moses looked at Khdir and said . . . what do you think he
said? *I wait for a reply.* (Kathy then says, "What did you
do that for?") *I then begin the ostinato drumming again
and chant to a plaintive melody the following.*

> The things that I do
> You may not understand,
> You promised not to question me.

(I then repeat the chant one more time.)

Ron   Moses looked at Khdir and said, "I'm sorry, Khdir, I
know I promised not to question anything. Just let me
continue with you, and I promise I won't question you
again." Khdir nodded his head. And so . . . they walked
on.

(Walking music begins . . . this section lasts a little longer than the
first as the group is now being more creative with the beat, except
for Vivian, who continues with the steady quarter note beat on the

wood block. I then return to the ostinato and each member fades out.)

Ron   As the sun was rising high in the noon sky, they continued down the road. In the distance, they saw a young traveler approaching. As he drew near, Khdir offered him no sign of greeting, but instead, pulled out a dagger and stabbed the young man . . . dead.

(Ostinato stops.)

Ron   Moses looked at Khdir and said . . .

(I pause, looking at the group for the answer.)

Vivian
and
Kathy   "What did you do that for?"

(I then begin the ostinato again and chant the melody, "The things that you do, etc." At the end of the chant I continue.)

Ron   Moses looks at Khdir and says, "I'm sorry Khdir, I know that I said I wouldn't question you. I promise I won't do it again." And so . . . they walked on.

At this point, the group begins to play again in a similar fashion to what they did earlier. Vivian again stays with a steady quarter note beat as the others experiment. Upon returning to the ostinato pattern, the walking music comes to a close.

Ron   It was getting close to evening, and the sun was moving into the west when they happened upon a city that was surrounded by a huge wall. Now, it has been said that robbers once roamed these lands and invaded the town on several occasions, so the people of the town built this wall to protect themselves. Now, we have not seen robbers in these parts for many years, and this wall now served no real purpose but to keep the villagers inside. So

Khdir walked down to the wall and pulled out a crystal
bowl similar to that which is in front of us.

(My drumming stops. I position myself in front of the quartz
toning bowl.)

Ron   He began to play the bowl in this manner.

(I begin to play the bowl, making it get quite loud. The resonance
of the bowl lasts for 30–45 seconds. As it decays, I continue with
the story.)

Ron   And with this sound, the wall around the town began to
crumble, the mortar between the bricks became dust, and
the wall fell. So Moses looked at Khdir and said . . .

(This time all the members join in and say, "What did you do that
for?" I begin the ostinato pattern again and chant the previous
melody.)

Ron   Khdir looked at Moses and said, "Three times now you
have questioned my actions when you had promised me
that you would not. So we can no longer walk on this
same path together. But this I will do for you, this I will
tell you. When we came upon the fishing village where I
drilled a small hole into their boats so that they would
sink, you could not see behind those mountains of the
harbor. Behind those mountains were pirates coming to
rob and burn the town. When they came around the
mountain to the harbor, they saw no boats and thought
that the village was deserted. So they passed it by. By
now, the towns people have already raised their boats
from the shallow harbor floor and repaired the small hole.
Now they can fish again. Then there was the young man
walking down the road that we met. He was on his way to
kill another that was about to marry. The family of this
young man believes in what is greater, and I have saved
them from the shame that would have been brought upon

them by their son. They can now have another child who will be upright and righteous. And this last village with the wall, you could not see that there were two orphan boys who were living on the outskirts of the town by the wall. Their father, who had died a while back, had buried treasure under the wall. When the wall fell, this treasure was revealed to the young boys who now can have what was due to them." And with that, Khdir walked away from Moses. Moses stood and watched Khdir walk into the sunset, and as he did, he hummed this melody.

(I then hum the chant melody that I had been singing earlier. I invite the group to hum with me and they all comply with the request. As the humming ends I also fade out the ostinato. At this point the session continues with this ending.)

Ron   There are four ways in which we *learn* in this world. (I change this from the beginning of the story where I say "hear.") Some of us learn from the sounds of our feet against the Earth, and it sounds like this. (I play the drum with a flat hand against the drum head.) We often call this learning from experience as our feet cross this Earth. Some of us learn from the sounds of the fire . . . the sparks of the fire. And that sounds like this. (I do a rim shot with my index finger.) As we learn from the fire, we often get burned . . . and so it's called . . . getting burned. And each burn leaves a scar. The only healing from burns is through time and forgiveness. Some of us learn best through the wind, and it sounds like this. (I run my fingertips in a circular motion over the drumhead.) We learn by catching the words of others in the wind, we learn from what they say. Sometimes they talk about their experiences, sometimes they give advice. All of us are searching for the fourth way, which comes up from the depth of the pond. It is that which comes from our soul, and it sounds like this. (I hit the center of the drumhead with my thumb.) Each one of us comes into this world knowing one way best to learn, and that with the others takes us through life. When you put them all together, they sound like this.

(I demonstrate the pattern I was using at the beginning of the group. I then bring the telling of the story to the end with a final beat. I pause for a few moments and examine the affect of the clients.)

Ron   That's the story.
Mark   I feel like I'm someplace else . . . I'm so relaxed.
Kathy   That was definitely neat.
Vivian Wow . . . what a story!
Ron   What I invite you to do now, is to think of how you have learned in your life. Have you learned primarily through your feet and experience? (I demonstrate on the drum again the flat hand against the drumhead.) Have you learned primarily by getting burned? (I demonstrate the rim shot.) Have you learned through hearing other people's words through the wind. Learning from their experiences or advice? (I demonstrate the wind.) Or, have you been able to learn primarily from your soul? (I play the drum with my thumb bouncing off of the center of the head.) So . . . who would like to go first?
Bill   I'll go first. I've learned primarily by getting burned. (He plays 4 strong rim shot beats. As he does his affect changes and he begins to look very contemplative.) I'm an alcoholic. I've hurt many people around me, my wife . . . my kids. But most of all. . . . I've burned myself as I am the one responsible . . . and I keep on burning myself.
Ron   It's sounds kind of like being a victim of your own behavior.
Bill   Yeah . . . that's right. I can't be any good to those around me until I quit hurting myself. I've been hurting myself a long time.

His affect at this point has definitely changed from the beginning of the group. He appears to be getting in touch with some of his feelings. I decide to ask what is happening.

Ron	Bill, what's going on right now with you?
Bill	(Long pause as he slowly stops playing drum.) I never really thought of it this way before. I've always wanted to blame others for my drinking. I'm just seeing this a little differently.
Ron	And . . . how are you seeing it?
Bill	Differently . . . I don't really know how to say it . . . just differently. (He then pauses about 30 seconds, almost as if in a trance. He then looks up.) So . . . that's it . . . who's next?
James	I'll go. (He begins to play the drum with a flat hand against the head.) I guess I've learned from my feet. My experience in life . . . I've always had to do for myself. One of the things about experience is that you're supposed to learn from your mistakes. But I haven't learned. I've made the same mistakes over and over again. And so now it's time to really stop, and learn from my experiences.
Ron	What are you learning?
James	(Long pause.) Well . . . I guess . . . that if I keep on drinking . . . I'll lose my family.
Ron	You used the word "guess" in your statement. Are you guessing that you'll lose them, or are you certain?
James	I'm certain. They've said they can't take it any more. I'm certain . . . that's why I'm here, to stop the drinking.
Ron	So . . . to stop the pattern, to learn from experience, what must you do now?
James	In group, we've talked about how it's one thing to stop, and get in the Program. But we also are starting to look at how I feel about this and . . . I guess . . . my life.
Ron	So, are you guessing again about your life?
James	Yeah . . . I guess so . . . there I go again.
Ron	So maybe there are a lot of questions that need to be explored and answered . . . since you guess so much.
James	Yeah . . . you're right. (He passes the drum to Vivian.)
Vivian	(Vivian initially struggles with trying to figure out how to hold the drum. She then slowly and tentatively hits the

rim as a sign of being burned. She does this in four slowly metrical beats. She has a tear running down her cheek.) I've been burned . . . and the scars are so . . . so deep . . . I don't know how to forgive . . . I'm so angry . . . so ashamed.

Kathy   (Handing Vivian a tissue.) It's OK . . . It's OK . . . It's not your fault.

Vivian   I don't know what to do anymore . . . they took it all away.

Kathy   I know honey, I know.

Vivian   I'm so sad . . . (crying).

When people are so emotive in a particular moment, they need to experience that moment, no matter how much it hurts or is painful for the therapist to watch. Experiencing the moment of emotion is critical to the healing process. So at this point, the group becomes a safe place for her as she cries.

Ron   It's difficult to feel these things . . .

Vivian   (Slowly) Yeah . . . That's all for now. (She passes the drum to Kathy.)

I remember earlier in the group when she was being resistant to the whole idea of playing instruments. I think that her brief verbalization is enough for now; she has initiated a change by passing the drum to Kathy, and I need to respect what she has done as well as the pain she is in.

Kathy   (Plays the sound of the wind, she also has a tear running down her cheek. She does not cry much, just a tear or two. As she speaks she is gazing at the floor.) I can remember my mother telling her friends what a wonderful child I was. Then, when we were alone, she would yell and scream at me and tell me how worthless I was. I couldn't figure it out. Why would she say those things and then yell at me? I still can't figure it out. The story made me cry, and I don't understand that either.

Ron   What part of the story made you sad? (Long pause.) The little boys that were orphans . . . I felt like they were so alone.

I first think of the connection that Kathy might be having with her own two children, and perhaps feeling that she is abandoning them. But on a deeper unconscious level, I think that the two boys are representing her feelings of emotional abandonment from her own parents.

Ron	Do you feel alone?
Kathy	Yeah . . . I feel very alone. I just want to figure this whole thing out . . . I haven't thought so much about my mother in a long time. She wasn't there for me . . .
Ron	Kind of like the little boys and their father.
Kathy	Yeah . . . they must have felt so alone.
Ron	But in the end they had riches that they never knew about, didn't they? And how did they get to those riches that were so buried?
Kathy	(Pause) The walls had to come down?
Ron	(Nodding)
Kathy	The walls have to come down . . . I think I understand.

That the wall represents her need to open up and discuss her pain in a group setting is one way to look at this. Another is that she needs to take the walls down for her own introspection. She also needs to be more open to the possibilities that can be opened for her in her life.

Vivian	Kathy, underneath all your pain is a beautiful person . . .
Michael	Yeah, Kathy, we know you are beautiful, you just need to find it for yourself.
Kathy	I guess . . .
Ron	There's a lot of guessing going on around here. (Members of the group laugh. Kathy passes the drum to Mark.)
Mark	(He takes the drum and at first seems to look at it seriously. He then plays the walking beat with a flat hand; he then makes the sound of the wind and finishes with the burn stroke. As he finishes, he looks up at the group with

	a big smile on his face.)

Bill   What was that!!

Mark   (With a bit of laughter in his voice.) Well, I was walking
        along thinking everything was OK, looking for my soul.
        (As he speaks he plays the walking stroke on the drum in
        a constant rhythm. He then changes to the wind stroke.)
        Then, all of a sudden, a big wind comes up making the
        walking very difficult for me, kinda like a storm. (He
        then starts with the burn stroke. He has a big grin on his
        face.) The storm was so strong that it burned me, and so I
        am here. (He stops playing.)

Vivian Mark, you're crazy (jokingly).

Mark   That's it.

Ron   That's an interesting story.

*At this point, I have to make a decision on how to handle Mark. He
didn't follow the instructions as presented and as the others have
done. This is also following in line with what he has been doing in
most of his groups, which is minimizing the problem. Not following
the rules is a behavior many antisocial-personality individuals
engage in. Getting into the inability to follow the rules may not be
the best approach at this time. I decide to explore the story, as that
is what he has presented. Not following the rules is a way of
avoiding the expression of feelings, especially if I focus on that.*

Ron   Can you tell me the story again with a little more detail?

Mark   Sure. (He begins playing the drum again.) I was just
        going on in my life, not causing anyone any harm. The
        wind comes up and that's my involvement in drugs. I get
        burned by the drugs and now I have to get off of them.
        That's all.

*With this he still avoids detail and also avoids the responsibility
for his own behavior, he blames the drugs for his getting burned.*

Bill   So you have a problem with drugs?

Mark   That's why I'm here.

There seems to be some friction between Bill and Mark. I get the sense that Bill is tired of Mark's lack of responsibility as well as commitment to the program.

Ron	Mark, your story seems to have three parts to it. The first is life is going along fine. The second is involvement with drugs. And the third is being in the hospital because of the drugs. Do you think that is an accurate summary of the story?
Mark	Yeah.
Ron	What is missing?
Mark	What do you mean?
Ron	Well, when someone tells a story, the story will have parts such as yours. What other stories have that yours seems to lack is connection of or between the parts. For example, you say your life is going along fine, then there are drugs. In my experience, there is usually a reason someone starts using drugs, yet you left that part of the story out. You also left out how exactly you were burned by the drugs. You left out important information.
Bill	He seems to do a lot of that.
Mark	No I don't (defensively).
Vivian	Sure you do, Mark. We all spill our guts, and you just sit back.
Mark	I talk all the time, I talk in group.
Bill	But you don't say much. Or at least we don't learn much about you from what you say.

(There's a long pause in the action.)

Ron	Mark, what do think the group is saying to you?
Mark	I'm not sure . . . that I don't talk much . . . or . . . I don't know (he seems frustrated and defensive).

Once again, I have to make a choice on what to pursue with Mark, to talk about what the group is saying, which seems to bottle him up, or to focus back on the story. I choose to focus back to the story.

Ron	Let's go back to the story. Do you understand what I was getting at regarding the connection between the parts?
Mark	Yeah . . . I think so. (Long pause.)
Ron	Can you fill in the parts we need?
Mark	I don't know. I got into drugs 'cause it was fun and made me feel good. If I wasn't into drugs, I wouldn't have lost my job and ended up here. That's it. Next person. (He says this abruptly and passes the drum to Michael.)

Here he becomes very controlling and takes the focus off of himself, taking charge so that he doesn't have to reveal more. This is a pattern he has developed well in groups, so once again I have to make a decision. Has he said enough and we reflect on this later, or do I confront him on this pattern of behavior? Knowing that time is also a factor, and there is more left to be discussed from others and in relationship to the meaning of the story, I decide to move on.

Michael	(He plays the wind pattern.) All my life, I have let others tell me what to do, what I should be . . . it's time to grow up. It seems that I could never please my family, no matter how hard I tried, I could never be what they wanted me to be.
Ron	And what is it that you want to be?
Michael	I don't know, I feel like I don't know who I am anymore . . . I don't know if I ever knew who I was . . . I just tried to be . . . what he told me to be.
Ron	He?
Michael	Yeah, my father . . . no matter what I did, I didn't do it right. I remember . . . (long pause, he is staring at drum) one time when I was maybe 10 or 11 . . . we were fishing, and I was trying to bait my fish hook. He kept showing me, and I thought I was doing it right, he finally said, "If you can't bait the hook, how are you going to do anything in life?"

As he sat there, I thought of what he must have been reliving at that moment. The sense of failure, sadness. How at such a young age he was being set up. Some children can adjust and still succeed after such experiences, and others may not, but for either child the experience at the moment is emotionally devastating. So what do you say at this moment? Do you focus on what they have accomplished in life , even if it was a small accomplishment? Do you ask them to say more? Do you connect them with another group member who is going through the same emotions? Do you sit there with them and just let them experience the emotion, the mood of where they are? These are difficult questions to answer and really depend on what you feel is most beneficial for them at this time. When someone is so involved in the moment, for this group, I let them stay in the moment, especially Michael, who didn't need me to tell him what to do or feel, people had been doing that for him all his life. So, we sat for about a minute, then he looked up at me, with almost a tear in his eye.

Michael	I feel kind of like Moses, I don't understand my life. That's one of the reasons why I am here . . . I need to understand who I am.
Vivian	I know what you mean, I feel lost, trying to find answers.
Ron	(Michael hands me the drum.) Sometimes, the answers take time to find. At other times, they come in quick little connections. Answers come through letting us feel, and then exploring the feeling, talking about it. In this process, we have an inner compass that sometimes needs help in finding direction like that of Moses, trying to find a way home and often not understanding the way. (Pause) So . . . now that you have all shared how you have learned in your life, let's take a look at what you thought the story meant. What did you think it meant? What was the moral?
Mark	Everything has a reason, even if bad things happen.
Vivian	Yeah, but, we don't understand why things happen, unless we look for the reason.
Kathy	I'm not really sure . . . bad things happen, and we don't understand why they do . . . but things in life don't always have to make sense. Things can just happen.
James	I guess what they say, there is a reason why things happen, but we don't necessarily know why these things

| | happen. I think that if we trust God these things will work themselves out. |

Bill   Sometimes, the worst things that can happen to us are the best that could happen, because we learn from them. I've self-destructed so many times, not knowing why, and that's why I am here, to find out why, so I guess it's to find out why bad things happen, they only have meaning if you can figure out why, or . . . something like that, to learn from them.

Michael   It's like they said, you can't accept things at just face value, you have to look behind . . . or below the surface . . . you can't judge a book by its cover.

As I listen to group members tell of what the story means to them, I also recognize the words that they utilize for their description. Mark used reason and bad together, and this is indicative of much of his life. He has engaged in many behaviors that at an internal level he sees as bad, yet without reason. To find reason, he will have to get involved in feelings, which he avoids at all costs. Vivian wants understanding and reasons in her life and is on that quest as she is being more in touch with her feelings. Kathy is continuing to try to make sense out of the abuse inflicted upon her. There's almost a reluctance to accept that she has no control over what people say or do to her, but she has a choice to stay in the environment or not. James is beginning to trust in his Higher Power, which he views as God. He continues to have a positive affect and sense of purpose through the group. Bill struggles between feelings and logic, he feels that meaning can only really come through logic. This has been a theme for him throughout the group, especially evidenced by his playing his portion of the improvisation in patterns. He finds meaning in logical sequence, yet this also keeps him from his feelings, which may, at this time, not easily be figured out. Thus, he can avoid them through intellectualization. Michael really has a little different approach to the story, but he discounts its worth with the phrase "It's like they said." This is typical for him, in that he has a difficult time accepting that a worthy thought or action may come from him alone, not because of what others say.

Ron	You have heard me speak of Jung before. It is his feeling that the characters of fairy tales and stories are actually all representations or symbols of parts of ourselves. They are parts of our own mind. So . . . if you were now to look at the characters or scenes of this story, and think of them as being a part of your own mind, or your own behavior, what would they mean? What would they represent to you? (There is a rather long pause.)
Ron	Do you all understand what I am getting at? That which you think of as Moses or Khdir, or any part of the story, can actually be a part of you.
Bill	Khdir is my action, and Moses is my logic.

This response catches me somewhat off guard, as I really don't get what Bill is saying. It seems off the mark from what I believe the story to mean. I must accept, however, that this is how he sees it. Once again, his move towards logic enables him to stay out of his feelings.

Ron	I'm not sure what you mean . . . can you tell me a little more?
Bill	Moses, the logic part of me questions all that I do, while it is the Khdir part of me that does things.

Bill has successfully taken the story to a very superficial level, one that he can successfully intellectualize on its most basic level.

Ron	So, if I understand you correctly, Khdir is that which you do, the external part of you, and Moses is the internal questioning part, is that right?
Bill	Yeah.

Again, a choice needs to be made, do I try to get him to see what I view as the meaning of the story, or just accept this as it is, and let the group take its course. I need to go back to basics for just a moment. "Any response that is given is valid." It is not my job at this point to correct him, but rather accept his answer. I let the group take its course.

Ron	(Slowly) OK, next?
Mark	Moses is that part of you that knows you shouldn't use, he knows it's wrong, but he just can't seem to stay away from it.

This comment from Mark seems to indicate that he is starting to look at his problem. He utilizes the word 'you' instead of 'I' in regard to using. This shows that he still is not internalizing his problem, but it is a step in the right direction.

Michael	Our soul is like Khdir. It is trying to lead us to a sense of health, but we like Moses don't understand this because we have been involved in so many self-destructive behaviors we don't know what is really going on. Moses doesn't quite get it, and through much of my life I feel like I haven't quite gotten it.

Michael is also really starting to look at himself a bit differently. His ability to understand there is a definite difference between healthy and unhealthy behavior, from an objective perspective, is a good sign. I feel that the Archetype of the Self is being aroused.

James	Khdir is my higher power, and Moses is all that questions the higher power when it should be accepting it.
Kathy	I still relate to the orphans more than anything else. I feel like I really had no parents, or at least parents that were real. Khdir . . . I think . . . is that part of me that I am, my real soul.
Ron	You use the word "real" a lot. What is real for you right now, Kathy?
Kathy	That I am here right now. That my life has been screwed up, that is real.
Vivian	I relate to the part of Moses questioning Khdir. I'm kind of confused whether Moses really knew if Khdir was God or not, because if he wasn't God you should question someone who is doing those things to others. What the

meaning is behind those things. So . . . I am Moses, not getting the reason for the bad things that happen in life. I don't know who Khdir is for me. Perhaps he is the inner strength in me, the will to survive . . . which could be the answer, but it doesn't make sense to me, at least not yet.

After all have given their associations with the story, I usually do some kind of summary that leads us into the end of the group.

The End

Ron   You all have wonderful insights as to the meaning of the story as well as how it relates personally to you. I was particularly taken with Michael's thought that Khdir is that part of us that is trying to lead us to health, and sometimes as he leads us to the concept of health, we have to experience difficult things along the way. It reminds me of taking really bad tasting medicine so that you can get better, these tough experiences in life are like bad tasting medicine, but without them we can't grow, or get better. We all have an inner guide within us, whether or not we pay attention to it or not is our choice. Khdir is part of all our lives. So, with that, our group is coming to an end. As I do in all my groups, I'll pass the harmony ball around, and as you hold it I invite you to tell the group what you will take with you from this group. Who would like to be first?

With this approach to the ending, I let each one speak freely without interruption from me. This is an important time for the group members, as they have a chance to reflect on what they have said and what others have said that might have influenced them. They usually roll the harmony ball in some way in their hands, and as they do a pleasant melodic chime comes from it. When they are finished with what they have to say, they roll the ball to the next member.

Michael (He begins with a big sigh.) What will I take . . . that I need to continue to focus on my own growth and to try to find out what I really want. This group really made me think about how much I've listened to others in my life and get lost in what they say. (He rolls the harmony ball to Vivian.)

Vivian   I think I am a little more accepting of this whole concept that there has to be a reason why things happen . . . wait . . . is that what I want to say? I'm not sure. I, like Moses, question the pain, but I may not find out the reason why it happened. So, I will have to deal right now with the pain.

James   Trust your higher power and stay with the program. I also learned how to play music in a group, and I really enjoyed that.

Kathy   I learned that I have a soul that is real. It is part of me, it is mine. I need to listen to it more closely. I also need to start letting some of my walls down so I can discover my riches.

Mark   I learned that I shouldn't use any more and not be like Moses who wants to use again like when he asks the questions. (This was said in a hurried fashion.)

Bill   This group was fun and made me think. What I learned was I need to be aware of what the cost of using drugs again will be. I don't need to place the blame on others. I need to be responsible for my own actions, which I have thought about before, but now it is clearer for me.

Ron   I want to thank you for participatiing in the walking music of the story. I also ask you to think about these things you've said here today. Remember the feelings of playing in the group as well as those insights you have gained. So, I'll see you next time.

FINAL THOUGHTS

I believe that the story reached the clients on different levels. On one level, they were able to look at what the story could offer them on face value. This was noticed when I asked them for the moral of the story. On another level, various parts of the story resonate for each client differently. For each client, this meant something on a deeper, more unconscious level was occurring. The archetypes were being aroused at this level and stimulated by aspects of the story. In discussion of what part of the story had its greatest effect, this can be noticed. For example, Michael is beginning to get in touch with the concept of wholeness and health through his comments on Khdir. He has begun to view his recovery in a different light because of this group.

Along the same lines, the story can become a catalyst for memory, as is seen with Kathy. She relates to the orphans and begins to discuss memories of her mother. Through the brief discussion, there is also recognition that there is hope for her after the pain.

Music played a role: in establishing a mood for the story; as a medium for the clients to be more involved in the story; as a means to express aspects of life; and as a bonding vehicle between the group members. What seemed most powerful was the playing of the hand drum solo by clients as an expression or extension of themselves. It provided for them a nonverbal way of communicating to the group something about themselves–their own personal story. The playing was a vehicle for them to express something for themselves, in a way they have never experienced before, something about how they learn in their life.

This session was just one aspect of their road to recovery. The following week Kathy, Vivian, and James all informed me that they thought about the session several times during the week and what it meant to them. Kathy and Vivian then went into a rendition of the chant:

> "The things that I do, you may not understand.
> You promised not to question me."

(With choreography.)

Chapter 7

MUSIC AND IMAGERY: AN OPEN DOORWAY

Heard melodies are sweet, but those unheard are sweeter.

—Keats, "Ode on a Grecian Urn" (1819)

When people hear their own voices recount their lives, their stories, the traumas and gifts they bear, therein lies part of the healing process. For in their voice is their melody, their own timbre and rhythm . . . a ballad being improvised. Hearing this ballad move from an internal voice, to the physical production, and then to the aural perception is a necessary component of the therapeutic process. So frequently in therapy, after clients find the courage to embark upon this process, their first comment is: "I can't believe I just said that, I've been wanting to say that for so long." The words and sentences that compose the stories are, in essence, melodies. At times, they are "sweet," as Keats would say; more often than not they are bittersweet in the telling.

In the above opening quote by Keats, he also says that those "unheard are sweeter." With this in mind, it is possible also to hypothesize that the "inner voice" as being sweeter, or even more bittersweet, in its expression. In taking this to another step, I propose that those words that represent conscious thoughts are sweet, as they relate and express something readily accessible from the psyche. But what is even sweeter then, is that which flows from the unconscious, that which is symbolic.

SYMBOLS, DREAMS, AND IMAGERY

In Jungian psychology, the unconscious makes itself known to the conscious world through symbols. Symbols, therefore, are an integral aspect of finding a balance between the conscious and unconscious. In Jung's book *Man and His Symbols* (1964), he says:

> . . . the symbol always stands for something more
> than its obvious and immediate meaning. . . .
> symbols, I must point out, do not occur solely in
> dreams. They appear in all forms of psychic
> manifestations. There are symbolic thoughts and
> feelings, symbolic acts and situations." (P. 41)

Jung approached symbols and their meaning with great
caution. He talks about the importance of knowledge, the
projection of the analyst, and the need to be complete in the
investigation of the symbol. One of the most important ways to
help find where the symbol is leading combines the above with a
sense of intuition imbedded in the therapist. As I mentioned earlier,
I think that intuition is one of the important facets in being
successful as a helper. Jung (1964) says this about the relationship
of intuition, therapy, and symbols.

> Imagination and intuition are vital to our
> understanding. And though the usual popular
> opinion is that they are chiefly valuable to poets and
> artists (that in "sensible" matters one should
> mistrust them), they are in fact equally vital in all
> the higher grades of science. Intuition is almost
> indispensable in the interpretation of symbols. (P.
> 82)

We encounter symbols throughout our lives. They are planted
within us at an early age, and according to Jung some are universal
and passed on genetically. Often, the role of the therapist is one of
guide, to help clients interpret their symbols. Understanding that
symbols do have personal meaning and that they may often be
connected to age-old myths, fairy tales, religions, or culture, the
therapist becomes very important in helping the client see these
being reborn within himself. The symbol is in the language of the
unconscious and that the power that lies within the unconscious is
great. Regarding this potential of the unconscious, Ackroyd (1993)
sums up Jung's view very well:

> It (the unconscious) aims at our well-being in the
> fullest possible sense; its goal is nothing less than

> our complete personal development, the creative unfolding of the potentialities that are contained in our individual "ground plan" or "destiny." This means not just healing, but wholeness. (P. 7)

Dreams come to us most often in the form of images. The images can range from accurately recalling real memories, to images that move and develop in a seemingly nonsensical manner. The images, however, form a basis of symbolic language. The image becomes the symbol, as well as the symbol inherently residing within the image. For example, an old man in ancient days would often be a man of wisdom and most likely a grandfather. Thus the old man image or dream will usually have an association with a theme revolving around wisdom.

Dreaming, however, is not the only means by which images come to us. They actually can come to us in varied states of consciousness. Fromm (1977) views altered states of consciousness as types of awareness that are different from the waking state. Thus, nocturnal dreaming, relaxation states, quasi-hypnotic states, and daydreaming are categorized as states of altered consciousness of varying degrees. Pascal (1992) also agrees that daydreaming and meditation are altered states of consciousness. Ackroyd (1993) states that meditation gives you the opportunity to explore "your unconscious mind by putting your consciousness into it. If, during your meditation, you visualize items that appeared in your dream, one after another, these may actually guide your conscious self in its exploration of the unconscious, leading it towards what it most needs to know at that time" (P. 33).

Jung used a technique called Active Imagination. In this technique, the client moves from the memory of a dream fragment into other images that one might conjure up in a relaxed state. Pascal (1992) says that active imagination is an "alchemical" work, in that it involves actively and consciously mixing elements from the unconscious with ego-consciousness for purposes of personal transformation and furthering our psychic evolution.

I believe that all that we do, all that we think, and all that we imagine have some purpose in our lives. These things are like the notes of a Bach fugue, all moving to some end purpose, a cadence that often serves not only as an end, but also a beginning. The images of dreams and even daydreams can be vital in telling what is occurring in the unconscious. In daily life, they often pass quickly and are unnoticed and thus unnoted. The group vignette that is given provides for the client to let the music stimulate images while being very relaxed. In the reporting of these images, there is the opportunity to take note of them and explore what they may mean. I believe that the images may have within them latent symbolic meanings, and also have the ability "instruct and inform the psyche by bringing forth the wisdom that already lies within the person. (Bruscia, 1991, P. 596)

GIM—A FOUNDATION

Music therapists need to be aware that unlike any other therapy ours has the closest link to the subconscious.

—Lisa Summer

Helen Bonny has laid the groundwork of the power of music to elicit images. Her book *Music and Your Mind* first published in 1973 and reprinted in 1990 is a concentrated work on this subject. From her work the "Bonny Method of Guided Imagery and Music," (GIM) was born. In the book, she describes the technique, which involves listening in a relaxed state or an altered state of consciousness (ASC) to selected music, in order to elicit mental imagery, symbols, and deep feelings arising from the deeper conscious self. The process fosters creativity, therapeutic intervention, self-understanding, aesthetic imprinting, religious and transpersonal experience, holistic healing, and personal growth (Bonny and Savary, 1973).

Bonny did a great amount of research as to what pieces and composers of the classical literature were effective in eliciting imagery. From her research she developed programs of classical music that utilized several pieces lasting anywhere from 25 to 45 minutes. These programs have been used successfully by many therapists throughout the years.

Helen Bonny was a true pioneer in the field of music and imagery. She developed the foundations of this approach, which many music therapists have drawn from and adapted to their own style.

MUSIC FOR THIS VIGNETTE

Visualizing to music while in an altered state of consciousness or in a very relaxed state allows for access to material of substance and power. Music, because of its relationship to the body and mind, and to history of humankind, has the unique power to energize and access the unconscious. The evidence of this lies within the stories of those who have experienced this, and by way of interpretation, find answers, reasons, and guideposts that help them in their path to wholeness.

My work with imagery and music is constantly maturing both personally and with my clients. From this work, I have developed a music program for small groups (ranging from two to ten members). The music is primarily popular style. It consists of bits of jazz, new age, and concludes with a classical selection.

Early in my music therapy career, I noticed how some pieces of music bring out similar images and adjectives from clients with the same diagnosis or similar extenuating circumstances. It initially began with clients' choosing adjectives to describe musical selections that were from the same group found in the Hevner groupings of adjectives (1937). The more I did this, the more consistent these descriptions became. I then began to ask the clients to describe some images they had to this, and they too began to take on many similarities. I realized that, although it was interesting that these images were similar in content, I really did not understand the full ramifications of the image. That is when I began a quest to find out as much as I could in regard to this area.

The choice of music, its order of presentation, and length all are extremely important factors. For this type of session, I have come up with the format of using instrumental music of varying styles and instrumentation, each selection lasting approximately two minutes in length. The session begins with a relaxation induction before the actual hearing of the music. The clients are asked to lie on their backs, and I take them through a relaxation exercise that enables them to get in a highly relaxed state.

Following this, the first selection is played. After the first selection, the clients report from their reclined position the images they had while listening to the music. They are given the option of keeping their eyes closed (which most clients do) as they report this. As they report, I keep a written record for each client of their images. After all have reported, the next piece of music is heard, and the reporting is done for that. This continues until all the selections are heard. The clients are then asked to wake up their bodies, return to a sitting position, and a time of investigating the images occurs.

The first selection was the beginning two minutes *Mexican Memories* by Michael Jones. This is a solo piano piece that is in a major key that moves from an initial sense of rhythmic freedom to a more grounded and somewhat slower rhythmic feel. I chose this piece initially for its sense of rhythm and the matching of the rhythmic feel of the induction. The more I used it the more I was convinced that it was an appropriate beginning place. The clients seem to be able to transition from induction to imaging to the music without much of a problem.

With *Mexican Memories,* clusters of images emerged on a consistent basis with the clients. The top three clusters of images that were evoked were as follows: a scene that had clients seeing or experiencing a form of water; clients seeing a child, at times a clear recollection of themselves, and at other times they couldn't make out who the child was; and the third was an image of someone playing the piano, which might have been them or someone on the stage.

In the first cluster, water is a focal point. Water has many types of meaning in images, I usually proceed from the viewpoint that water is attached to an emotion or psychic energy. How the water is experienced is quite important. For example, if the client images a river with a strong current, but does not get into the river, I consider that there is a strong underlying emotion (current) that may be unconsciously driving them and that they need to get in touch with (that is, get into the river). It might be that clients can't cross the river (get to the other side) because they are afraid of the current's (energy of the emotion) being so powerful. In that case, one must explore fear, and how to get across the river symbolically, and then find the appropriate relationship to reality. In one session, a client's image consisted of three rocks that led across the river. The rocks were strong foundations that led to the other side. After all the music was heard, we focused on the significance of the rocks, and the relationship to the client's life. The client came up with three principles and then made a poster with these three concepts: HIGHER POWER, TRUST YOUR INSTINCTS, KEEP THE FAITH. The client then concentrated on these principles throughout the inpatient stay. These were the guidelines on which to "cross over" emotional obstacles.

The second cluster image of the child is very significant for those dealing with childhood issues. These clients are often adult children of alcoholics, emotionally abused, physically abused or abandoned as children. Whatever the cause, most of the time there is need for resolution of some childhood issues. If there was a happy childhood and a real memory of happiness, the client may be wishing for a return to that former sense of innocence. It may be that the answers they are searching for can be found in the lessons learned as children.

I find that if clients are initially resistant to this process, or having a difficult time getting in touch with feelings and the unconscious, they will image the actual playing of the piano by someone. Or they may see themselves watching someone play— they become a distant observer of the concrete sound. If they have a real memory of themselves playing the piano at a young age, I would put it into the previous cluster.

There are many more images that have been reported by clients than just the above clusters. These clusters provide a sense of foundation for the following vignette. It would be far too much, and indeed, take another book, to explore all the other minor clusters that are also imaged for all the pieces that are being discussed.

The second selection departs from the first in instrumentation and style. From Leonard Bernstein's *West Side Story*, I use a two-minute excerpt from the piece titled "Cool." The excerpt is an arrangement for three guitars performed by the Falla Trio. The excerpt is taken from near the middle of the piece when there is obvious musical tension growing to a climax. I chose this piece because it was unlike that of the first piece in character and style. I felt that a departure would open up the possibility of going somewhere else symbolically and/or emotionally. What I did not anticipate was that many clients would be able to recognize the piece as being from *West Side Story* and therefore many of their images revolved around the musical.

For other clients, however, this piece evoked image clusters that do not relate to the *West Side Story* musical. The image of two dancers dressed in black with white gloves seems to occur the most. Nearly all the time, the clients do not see the faces of the dancers. Some might think that this is the meeting of the Animus and Anima Archetypes. Unless the client is specifically dealing with the Animus and Anima, I think that in this case it is more likely to be an association or an offshoot of real memory.

Of more significance is if the above image or any image that is linked with an emotional component of tension, anxiety, or fear. If this is the case, there is a strong possibility that the client has had one of these states activated (resonated) by the music. It might be that client is experiencing these things, either consciously or subconsciously. I will often have the client describe the feeling state and adjectives for the music. It is from this point of verbal description of the music, and its relationship to internal uncomfortable stimuli, that I can move into the relationship of life issues that may be related to the adjectives that described the music.

A third cluster is one of being chased or a sense of impending danger. There is often a stranger cloaked in darkness or hiding in the shadows lying in wait for something. This most often relates to two things. The first is that the client has had some sort of trauma and the shadowy figure is the perpetrator that has not yet been confronted. Or it might be a part of the psyche that the client fears or is not yet ready to meet. If it seems to be the latter, the client may be just getting involved with discovering the aspects of the Shadow Archetype.

The first two selections used instruments that were natural in sound, in other words, not needing to be amplified electronically in order to be heard. The third piece employs an amplified acoustic guitar as the primary melodic instrument with a backup group of drums, bass and synthesizer. This selection is the first two minutes of "Acoustic Highway" by Craig Chaquico. A quick and driving beat accented by a pleasant melodic line is the nature of the two minutes. The main cluster is of traveling via a vehicle or horse. The vehicle is most often a sports car, usually a convertible, driving along the coast. Being in a sailboat is another common image, as is riding a horse bareback. The clients almost always have a positive emotional reaction along with the image. There is often a sense of security that is heard in their voices as they describe the scene. At times, they may image characters that were part of previous scenes, somehow getting enmeshed in this image. I feel that this is an important middle point of the activity because it is setting them up for the final two selections. The mental travel in this piece is also part of a continuum of moving into deeper symbolic language. The metaphor of travel is in actuality what is symbolically occurring in the psyche. They are traveling and exploring into a deeper symbolic region or feeling state. The images to the next piece therefore become extremely important.

The fourth piece moves into a total electronically synthesized realm. The first two minutes of "River" by Enya has a less distinct melody and a recurring rhythmic feel. It has a full and lush-sounding texture throughout. There is no real cluster of images that are common for this piece. What is common, is that quite often the real issues that clients currently have to deal with and work through come up in a symbolic form. The move from selection three to four is a powerful move. The clients have settled into the session, the music has changed a few times, and this piece, for some reason, has many different images associated with it.

The last selection is approximately the last two minutes and twenty seconds of the "Firebird Suite" by Stravinsky. This selection starts with the pianissimo tremolo in the strings followed by the solo french horn melody and ends with the climactic finale. The main clusters of imagery center around the rising sun, mountains, flowers blooming, castles, and rebirth. The overwhelming emotional component that is attached to the images is one of optimism and triumph. In the overall processing and tying together of the images, which comes after everyone has described the image to the last piece, the client will often find strength and encouragement from the last images. On only rare occasions will there be highly negative images associated with this piece.

The sun is a powerful symbol, often representing the "true self," which is rising triumphantly over the darkness. It may also represent "new life" or personal transformation that is awaiting after therapy. Very often the mountains and the sun are paired in the images. The mountains are usually seen not as something to climb, but as something one is on top of. This may symbolize achievement, or mastery, or perhaps seeing life with a new perspective. Flowers are also Jungian symbols of the True Self. On the other hand, flowers might symbolize a way of looking at nature and the natural unfolding of life. The flower, after all, came from a seed that was once in darkness and very small. The blooming flower is the manifestation of light, water, and nurturing. The castle, which is a grand form of the everyday house, may also be a transformative symbol of the self. Clients will often describe in detail the beauty of these things. My job, as I see it, is to help the clients understand that they are in essence symbolically describing themselves. I place an emphasis on the positive movement of various aspects of the psyche, and I couple this with ideas of the internal healing process. Through this, the clients are enabled to gain insight and most importantly, hope.

SUMMARY

Jung felt that within the unconscious lie memories, thoughts, archetypes, and a great amount of emotional content. He promotes the concept that thoughts that have "lost their energy," are in residence in the unconscious (Jung, 1964). In various converations, he speaks of the ability to reach the unconscious through music (McGuire and Hull, 1977).

I think that what music does, in so many cases, is to re-energize the lost thought or memory, so that it becomes conscious. Now, this thought might be a real memory that has been previously forgotten, or it might indeed be part of the archetypal system that is coming through symbolically. I believe that the energy of the music has the ability to travel through different neural pathways to access such material. Thus, when someone is in a very relaxed state or an altered state of consciousness (where dreams often lie) and evocative music is introduced, there can be a rite of passage to such unconscious material. Music has the ability to energize those thoughts and memories that were once thought as being lost, and to restore them to consciousness, if not in original form, then symbolically.

REFERENCES

Ackroyd, E. (1993). A dictionary of dream symbols with an introduction to dream psychology. New York: Sterling Publishing Co. Inc.

Bonny, H. & L. Savary, (1973). Music and your mind. Barrytown, NY: Station Hill Press.

Bonny, H. (1978). Facilitating guided imagery and music sessions. Baltimore, Maryland: ICM Books.

Bonny, H. (1978). The role of taped music programs in the GIM process: theory and product. Baltimore, Maryland: ICM Books.

Bonny, H. (1980). GIM therapy: past, present, and future implications. Baltimore, Maryland: ICM Books.

Bruscia, K. (1991). Embracing life with AIDS: Psychotherapy through the GIM process. (PP. 581–602). Found in Case studies in music therapy. Ken Bruscia (Ed.). Phoenixeville, PA: Barcelona Publishers.

Chaquico, C. (1993). Acoustic highway. Los Angeles: Higher Octave Music.

Enya. (1988). Watermark. Geffin Records

Falla Guitar Trio. (1989). The Falla guitar trio. Concord, CA: Concord Concerto.

Fromm, E. (1977). "An ego-psychological theory of altered states of consciousness." The International Journal of Clinical and Experimental Hypnosis. 25, October, (4), 327–387.

Hevner, K. (1937). "An experimental study of the affective value of sounds and poetry." American Journal of Psychology. 49, 419–434.

Jones, Michael. (1984). Seascapes. Milwaukee, WI: Narada Productions.

Jung, C.G. (1964). Man and his symbols. New York: Dell Publish.

McGuire, William & R.F.C. Hull (Eds.). (1977). C.G. Jung speaking: interviews and encounters. Princeton, NJ: Princeton University Press.

Pascal, E. (1992). Jung to live by: a guide to the practical application of the Jungian principles for everyday life. New York: Warner Books

Chapter 8

GROUP VIGNETTE:
MUSIC AND IMAGERY

Dreams are faithful interpreters of our inclinations; but there is art required to sort and understand them.

—Montaigne

CLINICAL SETTING

The following clients were all in a locked-unit situation. They were allowed off the unit with supervision to go to twelve-step meetings, outings, etc. They would all be transferred within thirty days to outpatient programs or discharged with continued counseling. I had not worked with anyone in this group prior to this session. As usual, I spoke individually with each one of them prior to the group and let them know a little about music therapy, what we were going to do, and who I was. After doing this, all three of the prospective participants decided to attend.

THE CLIENTS

Marge—A 41-year-old black female diagnosed with depression. She has a history of panic attacks. Her parents were divorced when she was 9. She was emotionally abused by both parents and sexually molested by her father. She left home in her early teens and stayed in a home for girls. She got pregnant and had an abortion at the age of 14. She's been married twice, has a Masters Degree in nursing and has served as a chemical dependency counselor. She was admitted to the hospital because she became very depressed and suicidal. At the time of the group, she had been in the hospital for 10 days.

Sandy—A 44-year-old white female who is suffering from depression and has as history of alcohol abuse. She was admitted because she was having a very difficult time maintaining her current level of functioning, and her family feared for her safety. She has been resistant to therapy and defensive in many groups. She had been a poor historian for intake notes. She has had a history of difficulty in interpersonal relationships and has been married twice. Her parents were divorced when she was five, and she is an only child. She currently has a husband and two children She had been in the hospital for five days prior to this group. This is her first hospitalization.

Bob—A 41-year-old white male who has the diagnosis of major depression. He had recently overdosed on Dilantin and Ativan. He has had numerous hospitalizations prior to this. He has held several jobs in the past, is quite intelligent, but is currently unemployed and on disability. He came from an intact family, but his father was overbearing, emotionally abusive, and traveled extensively when Bob was a child. His wife of ten years died of cancer three years prior to this hospitalization. Bob had been in the hospital six days prior to this group.

THE SET UP

This group has minimal physical set up requirements. I usually will have adequate room lighting (not fluorescent) without being too bright. There are large pillows that are in a circle around a 14-inch quartz toning bowl. Prepared is a one-cassette tape with the selections that were described earlier. Between each selection is approximately five seconds of silence, which allows for appropriate places to stop and start the tape.

I keep pencil and paper close at hand. With these I record the primary images that are being reported or any other significant observations I might have while the clients are speaking.

This group is appropriate for those who have good reality orientation. Since the clients will be going through relaxation exercises to reach a heavily relaxed state and doing free imagery work, the prerequisite of being firmly in touch with reality is a must.

THE SESSION

Beginning—Warm Up

I had to bring the clients from the unit into the room where music therapy was to be held. On the walk to the room, I initiated conversation regarding things I already knew—such as asking questions regarding how long they had been in the program, where they were from, etc. Even though I know this information already, showing this type of interest in the client is helpful in establishing initial rapport. As we entered the room, I invited each one to take a couple of the large pillows and make themselves comfortable around the quartz bowl.

Bob   What's that? (gesturing to the bowl)

Ron   This is a one hundred percent quartz bowl. It's a toning bowl that, when vibrating, gives off the pitch of "B." It's really pretty neat and I like to start off all my music therapy groups with it.

Marge   It looks like a big salad bowl!

Sandy   How does it work?

Ron   Well, you first have to hit it with the striker and then the bowl starts to vibrate by rubbing the striker around its edge. I like to start off with this because since this is music therapy, and music is basically vibration in the air . . . this vibration helps prepare us for the session of music. So as I start the pitch, I invite you sit quietly, take some deep breaths, and let the sound envelop your being.

I use the word invite in the instruction quite purposely. Many therapists will say "I want you to . . . etc." which I feel puts pressure on the client to do what is "wanted." I try to avoid the words "I want" as much as possible. (I strike the bowl with the striker and excite the bowl to produce a long, powerful, and sustained pitch. As I terminate the exciting of the bowl, the pitch continues to ring.)

Ron   If you put your hands near the bowl like this, (I demonstrate) you can really feel the vibration through your hands.

Marge   This is really neat . . . I can really feel it (she closes her
          eyes, and I can see her physically taking in deeper
          breaths).
Sandy   I can feel it too . . . I've never seen anything like this
          before (she closes her eyes also and breathes deeper).
Bob   Yeah (he follows what the other two are doing and closes
          his eyes and takes in a deeper breath).

*As I observe them close their eyes, I assess that they are probably
comfortable in doing this action. Although I have witnessed some
patients do this group with eyes open for fear of closing them, this
group today seems to feel comfortable enough with each other, as
well as with me, in closing their eyes.*

*The tone lasts for about 45 seconds and slowly fades away. As it
does, the clients open their eyes and their affect appears less tense,
in fact Bob has a small smile on his face.*

Marge   That was really cool. I liked that . . . the sound at times
          seemed to bounce around the room and from ear to ear.
Sandy   Yeah . . . I felt that too, it was kinda weird, but I liked it.
Ron   It's a different way to start a group, isn't it?
Marge   Yeah . . . but its neat, I really feel kinda different . . . I
          don't know . . . it's hard to explain.

*The conversation continues about the bowl for about two to three
more minutes. The group, like so many groups, is fascinated not
only by the bowl, but also by their own reaction to its sound. This
relaxed talking and focus on the bowl is a nice way to warm up the
group, especially if this is the first time with them, as in this case. I
bring the discussion to an end about the bowl and begin to tell
them about the group that they are going to do.*

Ron   Well, like I told you on the unit, today we're going to be
          doing an activity that involves listening to music and
          creating some imagery. In music therapy, we do a lot of
          different types of activities . . . sometimes we play and
          create music, sometimes listen to words and music or
          even compose our own songs . . . and in today's group,

it's kinda easy for you since all you have to do is lie back, relax, and let the music stimulate images for you. How does that sound?

Bob   Sounds good to me . . . is this going to be like one of those relaxation tapes?

Ron   Not really. I know the type of tape you mean. It's purpose is to help you relax– a stress reliever.

Sandy   I have one of those tapes, it actually kind of drove me nuts!

Ron   I think that you'll find this group to be a bit different from those tapes, and maybe a little more beneficial. Before we start with the actual exercise, allow me to give you a little background for imagery work. One of the beliefs I have is that our dreams can give us messages from our unconscious.

Bob   I've heard about that, how your dreams really mean something . . .

Marge   I can't remember my dreams . . . so I guess I don't dream.

Ron   Everyone has dreams, but sometimes they are hard to remember. So, this activity works on the principle that dreams have meaning. Hopefully you won't fall asleep during it! What I have found out through this type of group, is that if you're really relaxed, and open to the experience, the images that you will have today with this music are much like a dream image. And being like a dream image . . . they may have meaning. I think that you should understand, that this may work with you and it may not . . . we never know till we try . . .

Bob   I'm ready . . . let's go.

Marge   So we're not supposed to fall asleep, but just get real relaxed?

Ron   That's it! Before we actually listen to the music, I will take you through a little exercise that will hopefully help you get relaxed and very comfortable.

Marge   What happens if we can't get any images?

Ron   I wouldn't worry about that, if there are no images, there are no images, that's all. If that happens for you, maybe you could just spend the time listening to the music, and take some time out to relax.

Through this whole warm up process, I am trying to create a an atmosphere of acceptance and minimal pressure. I am allowing them to see what kind of therapist I am by my voice tone, body language, and instructions. When clients suggest that they will not be able to image or have difficulty doing so, I try to take the pressure off of them by letting them know that it is OK not to force an image. I have found that initially these types of clients may have difficulty, but usually will have some images by the end of the group.

Marge   OK, that sounds good. I'm ready.

Sandy   I've never done anything like this before, but I'll give it a try.

Ron   Good . . . as I was saying earlier, the images are in a way– daydreams to music. They might make sense for you, or they might, like many dreams, make no sense at all. Dreams are often symbolic in nature. The images that you have might also be symbolic . . . I don't know, we'll have to see. But, if they are, they might have a symbolic theme that runs through all the images. At the end of the group, I will help you find the theme. OK? (They all indicate yes.) So, what is going to happen is this: you'll first get as comfortable as possible in this place with these cushions. I will turn the lights down low, so it is a bit darker in here, almost as if it were dusk. I will then give you some instructions that should help you relax; you will then hear five selections of music in various styles, all of them will be instrumental, and each one lasts about two minutes. As you listen to each piece, I invite you to let your mind imagine a scene to the music, almost as if the music became the background to the scene . . . like a movie. After each selection, I'll stop the tape, and from your reclined position, you'll each take turns and tell me what you imagined. At the end of all the selections, we'll look to see if there are any themes in your images. How does that sound to you? (Once again, everyone approves.) OK, why don't you try now to get as comfortable as possible, it seems to work better if you lie on your back.

I think that when you are doing groups with people who are not familiar with what you do, it is good to give them an idea of the overall flow of the group. This gives them a sense of security and often frees them up to be more involved.

This brings to a close the beginning or warm up part of the group. The group has got an impression of what we are to do and what is expected. I feel that this group has sensed that this is truly going to be a different type of group from others they have encountered in their treatment. The lights are dimmed, they get settled, and the middle part of the group begins.

Middle

The following instructions are given in a very relaxed manner.

Ron   As you get comfortable, I invite you to close your eyes . . . if you feel OK with closing your eyes, do that now (pause). Before we start listening and imaging, we'll go through a little relaxation exercise. First, become aware of your breathing . . . get in control of your breath by taking longer and deeper breaths (pause). You may want to let it become more rhythmic . . . by taking in a long breath to a count of 4, holding it for a moment and then slowly letting it out through your mouth to a slow count of four, then let the process begin again (pause). Breathe in 1 . . . 2 . . . 3 . . . 4 . . . , now hold it . . . and slowly let it out through your mouth 1 . . . 2 . . . 3 . . . 4 . . . and wait for a moment . . . now breathe in again and continue like this for a little while (pause). Now let your mind go down into your feet. Notice how your feet are resting . . . notice their position . . . now travel up from your feet through your ankles, through your legs and knees, notice how your lower back is resting against the pillows . . . feel the gravity of the earth slightly pulling you down into the pillows . . . let your focus now move up to your chest . . . notice the physical movement of your chest as it rises and falls with each breath . . . check your breathing . . . is it still slow and even? (Pause.) Let your attention now move through your shoulders, down your arms, and out to your fingers. Notice the position of your hands and fingers . . . let your mind go right out to the tip of your fingers and notice what they feel . . . what they are sensing . . . these are your extensors of life, they are how you often explore your world (pause). Now let your mind travel back up through your arms, through your shoulders, and up through your neck to your head. Notice the position of your head . . . notice how it is resting . . . notice how heavy it feels (pause). Now just let your mind examine your whole body, and let it relax (pause). Let your focus now move to all the sounds you can hear both inside the room and outside the room . . . let them all become part of your awareness (pause). Can you imagine the distance between you and these sounds? (Long pause.) In a few moments, you will hear the tape player "click" on. You will hear a piano playing music. When you hear the music, let your mind begin to wander to wherever the music might take you . . . just be with the sounds and the images. . . .

This is just one type of induction that might be used for this session. The above process takes about eight to ten minutes. I wait about another minute before I turn on the music. My voice is not as grounded as in giving earlier instruction, rather, it is a bit higher in pitch, quieter in volume, and a bit breathier in quality. I feel that this change in vocal structure and quality again signals to the group that something different is about to happen. The pace is very relaxed and loosely rhythmic, almost as if improvised. The induction is so very important in that it sets up the imagery . . . if the clients are not relaxed and entering into a quasi-altered state, then the group will probably not be an effective one for imagery. If they cannot relax, either the induction is not working, or they have their minds pre-occupied with issues that will not allow them to relax. If the latter is the case, it becomes a whole different group. The first piece is solo piano. It is the first two minutes of "Mexican Memories" by Michael Jones. When the selection ends and I turn off the tape machine.

Ron	OK . . . that was your first piece. You don't need to change your position if you are comfortable. If you wish, you can open your eyes, or leave them closed.

These instructions are given with the same type of voice quality as the induction with one change. My first statement, "OK . . . etc." has a little more presence to it, as I am indicating that the first image portion has concluded. It is necessary to bring the clients into a more conscious place. From here, they can tell about their images, hear others, and separate themselves a bit from the first selection.

Ron	So . . . who would like to start?
Bob	I'll start . . . I saw two people . . . and they were saying good-bye to one another. It was a man and a woman. They knew that this was the right thing to do, it was the right choice . . . they were sad, but knew that this was for the best.
Ron	Did you recognize the man or woman?
Bob	No . . . I don't think so.

At this point, I could really get into the different facets of this image with Bob, but because the group is only supposed to be an hour long, I want to move it along. As Bob tells me about his image, I write down the major points. I think also of how his wife has recently passed away and see some connections there.

Ron	Next?
Marge	I'll go . . . I first saw myself in my office, then it quickly changed to seeing my cousin's five-year-old little boy lying asleep in bed. I had just finished talking to his mother on the phone, and I was in my home . . . I really love my home.

These images move quickly from work, childhood, and then home. At this early point in the session, I think that there might be a theme of having to do work on childhood issues to get back home— or to the Self.

Ron	Uh huh . . . OK . . . Sandy?
Sandy	I had a hard time seeing anything . . . but when I finally saw something, I saw a concert pianist on the stage . . . playing the music.
Ron	Could you tell if the person playing the piano was a male or female?
Sandy	It was a man . . . dressed in a tuxedo.
Ron	Did you recognize him?
Sandy	No.

This is a common response when it appears that someone is resistant to looking at their issues or is a bit uncomfortable with this particular exercise. There is a detached view of what is going on in the image.

Ron	All right . . . you all did quite well with that . . . now we're going to hear the second piece. Remember, I told you that the music was in various styles and so this piece will be different from the last piece. Before I start the music . . . close your eyes and focus once again on deep breaths. When the music begins, let your imagination go with it.

I allow about a minute to pass as the clients concentrate on their breathing. Then the second piece is heard—The Falla Trio playing an excerpt from "Cool" which is part of West Side Story by Bernstein. The instrumentation on this piece is three classical guitars. This excerpt sounds increasingly chaotic in nature. It climaxes with percussive sounding hits on the guitars.

Ron	OK . . . that was number two . . . Sandy would you like to start this time?
Sandy	Sure . . . this is kind of weird. I saw myself snow skiing down this mountain slope, then it switched to me ice

skating on this frozen pond up in the mountains. The
weird thing about this is that I don't do either of these
things, but it felt really good to do them.

Ron   Are these things that you would like to do?

Sandy   No, not really . . . I never had a desire to do them . . . but
it was neat seeing them in my mind.

*I have found that the frozen water images often relate to someone's
being out of touch with their emotions. If water can be symbolic of
emotional content or process, when it is frozen it is out its normal
fluid state. It is hard and cold. For Sandy, this appears to be an
evolving theme in this session.*

Ron   OK . . . that does sound pretty neat! Marge?

Marge   I was once kidnapped by a cult . . . and kept against my
will . . . that was the first image, and it was real quick.
Then it changed to an old boyfriend that I had, and he
was playing his guitar. Then it got even stranger . . . he
was sitting under a tree playing, and all of a sudden I saw
his grandmother standing next to him.

Ron   So you had a real memory from a kidnapping, and then
an old boyfriend.

Marge   Yeah . . . I never really met his grandmother . . . I knew
that he was close to her . . . he would speak about her a
lot. He was sitting by a huge tree . . .

Ron   OK . . . anything else that you remember?

Marge   No, that's about all.

*Here, Marge moves through images quickly again. She goes from a
terrifying memory to someone she felt comfortable with–possibly
an emotional safety net to rescue her from the kidnapping image.
But then I think of the image of the grandmother. This is very
important. Here is a symbolic representation of the "wise old
woman" trying to get her attention.*

Ron   All right . . . Bob?

Bob   Well, all I could think about was *West Side Story* and the
Sharks and the Jets getting ready to rumble! Was that
from *West Side Story*?

Ron	Yeah . . . it was. Are you pretty familiar with the music?
Bob	Yeah . . . I loved the movie.
Ron	Out of curiosity, did all of you like this or dislike it in any way?

This is a question that I often ask after this piece. Many people have a very strong dislike of this segment of the music, since it becomes rather frantic. When someone has a strong negative reaction to it, I take note of it and ask why. They often reply with adjectives that have some meaning to their current life situation or problems.

Marge	Not really, at first it was weird, but then the image changed to something more pleasant.
Bob	I liked it!
Sandy	I thought it was OK music, I normally don't listen to music like that, but it didn't bother me.
Ron	OK . . . I was just curious. Let's get ready for the third piece . . . close your eyes and focus once again on your breath. (Long pause) This piece will also be a bit different from the ones you just heard . . . so in a few moments, you'll hear the tape player click on and the third piece will begin.

The third selection is just slightly over two minutes. It is Acoustic Highway *by Craig Chaquico. The instrumentation of this piece is different from the previous pieces. The primary instrument is amplified acoustic guitar, accompanied by drums, electric bass, and synthesizer. It is a quick piece in a major key that has a very strong sense of beat and a recurring melodic idea.*

Ron.	That was number three (long pause).
Bob	I really like that one.
Marge	I did too . . . I think . . . my old boyfriend came up again.
Sandy	That was . . . so much energy . . . I really liked it too.
Ron	Let's go one at a time . . . Marge how about you?
Marge	OK . . . well . . . It started with seeing my old boyfriend again. He was playing guitar and not paying any attention to me. I was just sitting there watching him play and

enjoying the music . . . but . . . he wouldn't notice me . . . kinda like I wasn't there. Then that image was gone, and I saw myself driving in a convertible down the coast . . . that was a great feeling . . .

The images of Marge are not as jumpy or quick. The image of the boyfriend ends with a feeling of being ignored. She then is in a car, which I view as her being transported to another level of her psyche.

Ron	Were you alone in the car?
Marge	Yes . . . I was.
Ron	What kind of car was it?
Marge	(Laughing) I think it was a Mercedes!!!

I will often ask this question, and it almost always gets the group to loosen up a bit more as they talk about a car that they probably have never owned, but now seeing themselves in.

Ron Do you know where you were driving to?

This is also a question I will always ask . . . what was the destination?

Marge	This is strange . . . I was driving to an AA (Alcoholics Anonymous) meeting.
Ron	But you didn't get there? You were still in the car driving at the end?
Marge	Yeah . . . it was a great feeling in the car.
Ron	All right . . . thanks . . . Sandy, how about you?
Sandy	Well I really like the music. It had such a great beat . . . just kind of made me feel good. Anyway, what I saw was an aerobics class working out. All the people were working hard . . . then my image switched to seeing people dancing.
Ron	Were you in any of the images?

This question is another often asked question. She is describing things that she sees, more from a distance as in the first piece. I think of the second piece where she sees herself in snow and ice.

Sandy   No, I didn't see myself . . . I was kinda there in presence, but just watching.

This is a response that I often get with people who think that they shouldn't be in treatment or who are having a difficult time getting involved with their true feelings.

Ron   I see . . .

I try to reply as much as I can with the same types of predicates or words the client has just used. In this case, she is using "see," which is visual predicate. I reply with the same. I could however have used a phrase such as "I get the picture" or something similar to this. This is based on Bandler and Grinder's Neuro Linguistic Programming, which is very helpful for establishing contact with a client, especially one like Sandy who seems to be keeping everyone at a distance. I will discuss Neuro Linguistic Programming further in Chapter 8.

Ron   Bob, you seemed to have a strong reaction to this piece.
Bob   Yeah . . . I really like it, and I had a powerful image with it. I saw myself climbing a mountain with my niece. As I got to the top of it I had an amazing sense of power. It was really fantastic.
Ron   You were with your niece?
Bob   Yeah . . . she's a professional climber and she's the only one that could save my life up there if something were to go wrong.
Ron   Is this a real memory?
Bob   Well I have climbed mountains with her, but not one like this, nor have I really had that feeling before. It was different from things I've done.
Ron   Did you see anything when you were at the top of the mountain?
Bob   No, not really, it was more of an experience . . . a feeling.

Ron   You seem really touched by this experience.

Bob   The more I think about it, the more it amazes me . . . it is really hard to describe.

I am moved by his image. He appears to be symbolically moving over obstacles, and he is willing to let a female help. She could represent his feelings enabling him to go through this, or she might be representational of a female therapist that he trusts.

Ron   Well then, let's just let that settle for a moment (Pause). Are we ready for the fourth piece? (Everyone acknowledges that they are ready.) OK . . . close your eyes again, and focus on your breath . . . just let your mind go blank as we get ready to hear our next selection.

(The next two minutes of music is "River" by Enya. This is primarily synthesized music with a defined beat, but not as rhythmically driving as the previous piece. The melody is repetitious in character.)

Ron   That was number four . . . who would like to start? (Long pause.)

Bob   I will. I saw myself as a little boy . . . I was at a lady's house that lived down the street. She was like a second mother to me. I was eating pie, and then I went out to play.

Ron   Was this a real memory?

Bob   Only of the lady, I don't know if I ever ate pie there.

Ron   Did you see anyone else as you went out to play?

Bob   No, I don't think so, I just know that I was going to play after the pie.

Ron   Can you describe what the little boy was feeling in this image?

Bob   Safe.

Ron   (Pause) Safe . . .

Bob   (Quietly) Yeah . . . safe.

Here again is a reliance on a female image. In this one, she is offering nourishment and safety, which is different from the female

*in the previous image. I let a little time pass to see if Bob will say
anything else about this image. Since he did not, I decided to move
on.*

Ron	Next?
Marge	I was a little girl . . . I was lighting candles . . . and I was telling a Christmas story. I went into the kitchen and ate potatoes.

*I find it interesting how in certain groups the clients will have very
similar images at the same time. Here both Bob and Marge saw
themselves as children, and both of them were eating something
during the image. Here, Marge has another image of a child . . .
remember that the first image also had a child image in it, along
with her home, which is again present here. Another important
aspect of her images is that this one comes directly after she sees
herself driving a car, a symbol of movement. This movement leads
her into this powerful image. Candles are important symbolically
in that they "shed light" on things. For centuries, candles were the
only way we could see in the dark. So what is she trying to see?
Another aspect is that she was telling a Christmas story. The
Christmas story has to do with birth under the most difficult of
circumstances.*

Ron	Potatoes?
Marge	Yeah, I have no idea why . . . kind of strange don't you think?
Ron	Well, it depends on whether the potatoes were good or not.
Marge	(Slightly laughing) I guess they were good, I didn't spit them out or anything. Does all this mean anything?
Ron	Maybe . . . we'll have to be patient till after the last song, and then we'll try to make sense out of it. Sandy, how about you?
Sandy	I had no image. I was thinking about what I was thinking . . . and didn't have an image.
Ron	What were you thinking about?
Sandy	Mostly thinking about not having an image. And just thinking.

Ron   OK . . . sometimes images just don't come.

Sandy   Definitely.

Ron   Did you like or dislike the music?

Sandy   It was OK, I don't have any strong feelings about it either way.

These statements by Sandy show her resistance to feelings. By intellectualizing she doesn't have to image or risk feeling anything. She seems to be tuning out the music, and also she will not let its presence stimulate feelings.

Ron   All right, we're almost done with the listening part of this group.

Bob   This is really great . . . I could do this all night!

Ron   Unfortunately, we don't have all night, and after this last piece, we will hopefully be able to look at all these things and see if they mean anything. So let's get ready for the last piece . . . close your eyes . . . focus on your breath, and in a few moments the music will start.

(The last selection is approximately the last two minutes of the "Firebird Suite" by Stravinsky. This piece is for full orchestra. It starts off quiet and gradually grows into a loud, strong, and rhythmic ending.)

Ron   And that's the last piece . . .

Marge Can I go first?

Ron   Sure . . . go ahead.

Marge I first saw an ocean . . . then I saw whales and dolphins swimming in and out of the water. Then I realized that I was in the water with them . . . swimming. And as the music got louder and louder, we swam faster and faster . . . I felt very free. As the music got close to the end, a man lifted me out of the water. . . . and he held me up over his head . . .

Ron   Did you recognize the man?

Marge No . . . it was so strange though, he was holding me up as if offering me to the sun or something. It was really very vivid.

Ron   It sounds like it was a powerful experience for you.

Marge   It was . . . I really enjoyed feeling like I was swimming with the dolphins, but then to be held up by the man, that was really something.

Here I feel is a strong symbolic movement toward her Animus—or male strength supporting her. It also reminds me of a father from an age gone by holding up his newborn. This all may have to do with an emotional rebirth or discovery.

Ron   It really seems like something . . . OK. . . . who's next?

Sandy   I'll go . . . this time I did have an image. It was of an angel that was floating in the sky . . . I'm not sure if the angel was me or not . . . I couldn't see the face . . . but what I got from it was . . . freedom.

Ron   Freedom?

Sandy   Yeah . . . freedom, like . . . I don't know . . . just freedom.

Ron   So, as you listened to this music, the first image that came to you was of an angel . . . and what was the angel doing again?

I will approach resistive clients this way at times, it is a way to see if they will give more information. I repeat part of the experience, and leave out some and ask for help in remembering it. Quite often clients will elaborate on what they have just said.

Sandy   She was . . . just sort of . . . there, I guess flying, although her wings weren't moving . . .

Ron   So the angel was a she?

Sandy   (Long pause.) Yeah (slowly . . . pensively).

Ron   You said that there was a sense of freedom with this image . . . do you know . . . well freedom from what?

Sandy   I don't know . . . (Pause.) . . . I really don't (affect looks confused . . . crossed up.)

Ron   The angel . . . did you get any sense of fear . . . or was she friendly.

Sandy   Definitely friendly . . . definitely.

Often angels are the bearers of messages and/or blessings. For Sandy, the message seems to be freedom. But freedom from what?

Ron OK . . . and how about you, Bob?

Bob I saw a young woman, I believe she was an American Indian . . . and she was leading a bunch a kids off of a reservation for the day. And that's about it . . . she was leading them off of the reservation.

Ron Almost like she was helping them find freedom . . . or safety?

Bob Yeah . . . probably both, it wasn't necessarily a happy scene . . . I'm not sure where it came from . . . but the kids were not in any danger when they were with her.

Ron So there was safety with this woman, and also with your niece, and also, perhaps, with the woman whose house you went to have pie with?

Bob Wow . . . I'm not sure what that means, but it is interesting.

Ron So . . . why don't we all kind of wake our bodies up slowly before we continue this discussion about the images. Slowly let your body come out of its rest period . . . wiggle your toes a bit, stretch your arms and fingers . . . OK. . . . everyone back? It has been interesting for me to hear all your images, and for each one of you, there is a theme or maybe even themes that have run symbolically through them. Since I already started discussing this a bit with Bob, let me continue with him. Is that OK with everyone? (They approve.) Bob, as you can already see there is a theme of safety, which is accompanied by the presence of a female. Two of the females you know, and the other one it seems that you do not know . . . is that right?

Bob Yeah . . . I can see where the safety thing comes in, the lady down the street was always so nice to me, I did feel safe there, it was a place to get away from my home.

Ron And you were also being fed there in the image. Being fed can be not only physical nourishment, but also something symbolic . . . being fed emotionally, or in

	security, or things like that. You also had images of two journeys . . . one up a mountain, and one off of a reservation, both are kind of a sense of accomplishment, which is power, or . . . maybe freedom. What do you think about that?
Bob	(Long pause.) Wow, that's kind of a lot to digest . . .
Ron	"Digest" is another food word—or being fed—could it possibly be that this is a time to be fed . . . emotionally . . . or opening up to that possibility?
Bob	I was just talking about that in group today . . . I'm starting to trust the people here, but I am not really sure on how to open up (pause). I'm not sure how to put into words that which I feel . . . it's hard . . .

Sensing that he is getting a bit stuck, I decide to intervene in a different way, one that seems to help clarify what is going on since the group is on a time limit.

Ron	Bob, let me try something with you . . . I am sitting outside of you now with all your images before me . . . I think I can see connections that you are having a hard time seeing. Let's pretend that I am actually like a little voice that is part of you, and I can help figure out the code to the images . . . as you listen, check to see if you think what I say is accurate . . . OK?
Bob	Sure.
Ron	There is something that I, meaning me—Bob, am trying to express. I feel that some of it has to do with sadness as in the first image . . . and I know that it is the right time to do this. I think, that through the process of getting in touch with the sadness, expressing it with people I feel safe with, working through it, almost like climbing a mountain, that I will be empowered and set free from the emotion that binds me. The key is, letting the emotion, or the emotional part of you, like the Indian at the end, lead you to this freedom . . . What do you think of that?
Bob	Exactly . . . that's exactly it . . .
Ron	You see, Bob, these images are all a part of you, they can

be just images to some music, or they can be a real part of who you are and what you need to do . . . it's up to you to decide.

Bob   I think that these are real, because how else would I feel so sure of what I need to do right now?

Ron   And what's that?

Bob   To trust my group, and . . . just say what needs to be said.

Ron   Part of that also, is to just feel what needs to be felt, and then tell what that feels like.

Bob   That's true . . . that's true . . .

The method of putting all the images together and talking to the client as if I were part of the client's psyche has been quite successful. Because if I am not near to what is going on with them, then, we go from there . . . which opens up more doors. In the first image that he had, he did not identify who the people were—I think it was part of his psyche saying he had to let go of certain things, and although this would be sad, it would be the right thing to do. All the women images were, I believe, Anima Archetype images leading Bob to finding emotional expression. In feeling the expression, they were letting him know that he would find release, safety, freedom, and power . . . all things that are there to feed a healthy psyche.

Ron   Marge, would you like to talk about yours?

Marge   Sure.

Ron   You actually have some similar images to Bob. Where Bob was imaging women, you were imaging men. You both also at one point, in fact to the same music, saw yourself as young children eating something . . . nourishing the child.

When possible, I try to connect some thematic concepts within the group. I find that this helps in the development of group trust and identity.

Ron   You also have an old woman appear, the grandmother, who we often might call the "wise old woman." Although she did not speak to you today, her presence seems to be within you, trying to either guide you or get your attention. The kidnapping, although only present for a moment, is also significant, as it may indicate unresolved issues with that event, or possibly your feeling very caught in this moment in time, almost as if you were kidnapped, or trapped against your will. The images of men may signify what we call the Animus inside of you That is in every woman there is a counterpart within her that is also man, and this counterpart gives her strength and courage to tackle things she might think she doesn't have the strength for. And, of course, the ending is so powerful, where this inner strength says "Rely on me to carry you through . . . I will hold you up victorious through these trials!"

Marge   (Big sigh.) It really makes sense . . . how do you do that?

Ron   Years of experience and reading . . . and . . . some intuition I think . . . which you also have . . .

Marge   Intuition?

Ron   Yes, and part of that is found within these images. Now that I've said these things to you, tell me, taking these concepts, do they fit with what is going on now?

As I have said before, these groups are in a time constraint, so I will often give an overall picture of the images and their themes. At the end I ask for feedback on whether I was accurate and whether or not the images might truly mean something for the client.

Marge   So within me there is strength?

Ron   Yes.

Marge   How do I get in touch with that?

Ron   Perhaps you are already in touch with it and it just needs to be consciously acknowledged . . . for example, what demanded strength for you today?

Marge   Well . . . in group I started talking about my childhood, and that is always hard . . .

Ron   So that took strength and courage?

Marge   Yes.

Ron   So, it is important for you to recognize that it is inside of

you and also within the realm of your possibility!
Sometimes it manifests itself without you knowing, and
at other times, you can call upon it . . . for you know it is
there, and, in fact you have seen it in your mind.

Marge   (Long pause.) This is so cool . . . can I ask you something
else?

Ron   Sure.

Marge   What about the first image where I saw myself in my
home . . . I really liked that one.

Ron   Yes, that actually might tie in with the imaging of
children, kidnapping, and nourishment. The home often
represents our psyche, or who we are. When you saw
your home how did it look?

Marge   It looked very nice, comfortable and clean.

Ron   Is that how it is in reality?

Marge   Well it's nice and comfortable, but not always clean . . . I
have a difficult time with that.

Ron   With what?

Marge   Keeping it clean . . . (long pause).

Ron   Marge . . . what are feeling right now?

Marge   Oh God . . . Oh God . . . (slowly, with a tear running
down her cheek).

Ron   Marge it takes courage to feel this, so let it be with you
now.

*I hand her some Kleenex. Sandy gets close to her and holds her.
This is a time of quiet support for a hurting member, I am there to
contain and monitor . . . even though she did not verbalize her
feeling, she expressed it. After a few minutes I come back in.*

Ron   Marge . . . you just made it through this . . .

Marge   I know . . . it's so hard.

Ron   There is a child inside you that needs your help, she
needs to be nourished and taken care of. In return, she
will bestow on you great blessings, and your home will
be cleansed and put in order . . . do you understand?

Marge   Yes . . . thank you . . . thank you so much.

Ron   (I nod in acknowledgment.) And so, we have one person

	left... Sandy.
Sandy	I don't know how you are going to make any sense from mine.
Ron	Well, yours is a bit different from the others. Sometimes we find ourselves in situations that we'd rather not be in.
Sandy	Boy, isn't that the truth.
Ron	Sometimes the situations are there for a reason, and we try with all our might not to be in them.
Sandy	What do you mean?
Ron	Can I ask you a question?
Sandy	Sure.
Ron	Why are you here?

Even though I know why Sandy is in treatment, I thought it appropriate and important for her to verbalize the reasons.

Sandy	My family was concerned about me.
Ron	Should they have been?
Sandy	What do you mean?
Ron	Did they have reasons to be concerned?

At this point I can see through her body language and tone of her voice that Sandy is starting to become defensive.

Sandy	Not really
Ron	Sandy... do me a favor... take a few deep breaths, notice the tension that is building in your body, try to breathe through that.

Sandy continues to look resistant.

Marge	Come on Sandy, give it try... it's not going to hurt you.

Marge coming in at this point is a key part of this exchange. Sandy had just been there for Marge, and there was a connection made, and now Marge was encouraging Sandy to become more involved in this process. . . after the encouragement from Marge, Sandy closes her eyes and begins to breathe deeply.

Ron	That's it . . . now just let each breath move through your body . . . and as it does . . . your mind will become more relaxed and open. (About a minute passes.) If you wish, keep your eyes closed and just think for a few moments about the question I am going to ask you before replying. Did your family have reasons for concern?
Sandy	(Long pause and then she quietly answers.) Yes . . . I guess so.
Ron	Yes . . . I guess so?
Sandy	Yes.
Ron	Sandy . . . your images are almost all from the perspective of being outside looking in, being detached, for in a detached world we don't have to get involved, and if we don't get involved, we don't have to feel, and if we don't have to feel, we don't have to hurt . . . but we also then can't feel the other side of the spectrum, which is happiness. Does this make sense to you?
Sandy	(Eyes open now, she tentatively answers.) Yes.

I wait to see if she'll offer more, but she does not. Maybe this is enough for one session, a small crack in the doorway. But then one more question comes to mind.

Ron	Did any of the images seem different, or out of place from the rest?
Sandy	Yeah . . . the last one.
Ron	Can you tell me about it again?

I ask for her to re-describe it, hoping again that she will give more detail.

Sandy	There was an angel, and she was just floating in front of me, I couldn't really see her face, but I get the sense that it was a she . . . and I don't know why, but there was a sense of freedom there.
Ron	You know it is said that angels were created with specific purposes in mind. Some are messengers, some musicians, some to keep warriors safe in war . . . could you call this the "Angel of Freedom"?

Sandy	Yeah . . . that's kind of a neat name.
Ron	And I think you said this angel seemed friendly to you?
Sandy	Definitely a friend . . . I could sense that presence.
Ron	Let me propose this to you, and it is just a thought . . . friendly angel images often mean there is something in the psyche that is watching out for you, something that is saying it's OK to do this or that because I am here to protect you. If this is the Angel of Freedom in your mind, why do you think it is there? What is her purpose?
Sandy	(Long pause.) I know what you are saying, but I don't get the purpose part . . . to be free?
Ron	Free from what, Sandy?
Sandy	(Long pause.) I don't know, I really don't.
Ron	OK . . . I think that is something to explore this week in your groups. (Pause.) Well, we're just about out of time. Before we close, I'd like to introduce you to this little harmony ball, which I end all my groups with.
Marge	That sounds so neat . . . I want one!!
Ron	We end the group by rolling it to one another, and when it comes to you, just hold it, experience the sound, and answer this question for me . . . What will you remember from this group? What will you take with you?

I roll the ball to Bob. As each client takes the ball and speaks, I try not to interrupt them in any way, nor do I really get into the processing of what they are saying. I've made it clear that this is the end of the group, and so this is their opportunity to add whatever closure they might need.

End

Bob	What will I take with me . . . well . . . that this is really cool, first of all, and that I need to trust my group, allow myself to feel things and express them to the group. That's what I'll take with me. (He rolls the ball to Marge.)
Marge	I have strength inside of me . . . I will survive this . . . I also have a hurting little girl inside that needs to be taken care of . . . (She rolls the ball to Sandy.)

Sandy   I guess what you're saying is that I am out of touch with feelings, and maybe don't express them well. I'm not sure if that is the case . . . but I'll think about it. (She rolls the ball back to me.)

Sandy once again refers to the concept of "think" instead of "feel." She also doesn't even mention the final image that was so archetypal in nature. Possibly she avoids this because to address it would mean she would be getting involved in the process of treatment.

Ron   What I will take with me from today . . . well . . . let's see . . . (pause) I guess I'll take the fact that I have had the opportunity to work with three courageous people today . . . and that each one in their own way . . . allowed the music to come in and just be with them for a small part of their day. That's what I will take with me . . . so . . . this brings us to the end of our group. Slowly get yourselves off of the floor and on to your feet . . . and we'll go back.

FINAL THOUGHTS

What happened Tuesday night? Bob just opened up in Wednesday's group and really did some good work. He said Tuesday night gave him the courage to do that. What did you do?

—Primary Therapist working with Bob.

I have found that this session can be relaxing, powerful, insightful, and fun. What continues to impress me is that clients, when you prepare them properly, can become so involved in this exercise. The more I do this activity, the more I see similarities in the images and themes that come out. This, I believe, is because so many of the clients are in treatment for similar reasons, and the archetypal unconscious is working in its symbolic way with all of them. This session, like music, may exist and be experienced on many different levels. When the therapist can truly be Present along with the music for the client, this group can be extremely effective. Within this framework, I see how music reaches places that only it and art can find. In those places, it resonates pathways that have often been lying dormant for much of one's life. From the depths of the psyche come, in symbolic form, questions, answers, and insights, that (like music) can be analyzed and/or experienced. When using knowledge and intuition as internal co-therapists, the therapist can help the client find significant meanings, and with this clients can choose new paths that they did not know or had forgotten. For Sandy, it was her angels, freedom, and caring. For Bob, it was finding the need and means to express feelings. And for Marge, recognizing that she has an inner strength and finding self-confidence.

Chapter 9

MUSIC THERAPY IN A RECOVERY MODEL

Problems are only opportunities in work clothes.

—Henry J. Kaiser

Charles Whitfield (1989) uses the terms Real Self, True Self, Child Within, Inner Child, Divine Child, and Higher Self interchangeably in his book *Healing The Child Within.* He states that this is who we are "when we feel most authentic, genuine or spirited." (P. 11) The significant others and institutions in our young lives help us formulate this part of us, which has a lasting impression on us throughout our adult lives. "When this vital part of us is not nurtured and allowed freedom of expression, a false or co-dependent self emerges." (P. 11)

Definitions of co-dependence are many. Some characterize it as a condition, others a disease. Whitfield (1989) feels that it is a condition that stifles our True Self, our Child Within. He defines co-dependence as:

> any suffering and/or dysfunction that is associated with or results from focusing on the needs and behavior of others. Co-dependents become so focused upon or preoccupied with the important people in their lives that they neglect their True Self. (P. 28)

On the other hand, Bradshaw (1990) sees it as "A disease characterized by a loss of identity. To be co-dependent is to be out of touch with one's feelings, needs, and desires." (P. 8) The thread that seems to unite these and other definitions that are offered in the literature is the loss of identity, loss of a sense of what one truly needs and how to get those needs met.

Many of the clients struggling with the issues of co-dependence, depression, alcoholism, chemical dependency, etc. are in a struggle to find their Real Self. This is a self that has been hidden, denied, or repressed, yet is a viable part of the psyche. The process of getting in touch with that part of us is usually painful and requires courage. The therapist acts as a support system and a guide while the client progresses through various stages of growth. The recovery model that I utilize in this process is the one described by Gravitz and Bowden (1985) in treating adult children of alcoholics and which Whitfield also expands upon. I have found that music can play an important role in each one of these stages. Through the music therapy experience these various stages can be identified and explored. The steps of recovery are as follows:

1. Survival
2. Awakening or Emergent Awareness
3. Core Issues
4. Transformations
5. Integration
6. Genesis (Spirituality)

1. Survivial

Survival, in its basic sense, means to outlive or continue longer than the event(s) itself. In essence, you then become the survivor of the event. You still exist, you are still alive. As a child, the many defense mechanisms and coping skills are used to make it through the trauma. Jung feels that the child is endowed with a great deal of survival instinct, as indicated in many fairy tales. As people begin to realize that they are survivors, there can be a great deal of pain and suffering, or to the contrary, feeling very numb. A state of emotional shock may be entered when realizing that it is time to begin the process of looking back before being able to look forward. Both directions are emotional unknowns for the survivor and can bring on fear and anxiety regarding the process.

Many of the clients I have worked with have already entered this stage of recovery. A client may have already seen the need to investigate his life, find meaning, and a new way of living as the goal. The client may not fully be aware of the ramifications of the journey toward the goal, but realize that it must begin because the way he has been living is not working. It is important to help the client identify with the concept of emotional strength so that the choice can be made to embark on this journey. The initial identification of strength often comes to people from the realization that they have survived the event(s).

2. Awakening or Emergent Awareness

The second stage of development is Awakening or Emergent Awareness. Understanding that one is a survivor does not necessarily mean total insight as to difficulties in life. This stage truly begins when there is a "trigger" that shakes up old belief systems, and strong emotional reactions may occur (Ferguson, 1980). This trigger can be brought about through many different musical activities. I have found the most effective trigger is through imagery to music activities, drawing to music activities, and at times lyric interpretation.

In vizualizing to music, many of the images that are generated by clients are ones of seeing themselves as a small child, usually alone or sometimes standing in the rain or by a house they think they might recognize. They may see themselves holding a baby or even a child resembling themselves. When people are at this point of emerging, they are like a bubble ready to burst. Words to a song, images they have drawn on paper or have imagined—all can reach down into the psyche and energize this movement to go further. As they come to realize the significance of the moment, image, or drawing, this realization triggers them into a feeling and dialogue of how things may not be what they seemed. This allows them into an entry point of feeling something that is real, which means that their True Self is being accessed. The range of feeling is wide— from anger to enthusiasm, excitement to sadness—but whatever the feeling may be, it is authentic and truly experienced.

It is at this point that the client must truly sense Presence from the therapist. The client is in need of safety and containment. There is an understanding that someone is there who will not abandon him and furthermore go through this process with him. It is a great risk for the client to proceed with this journey. It is at this time that relapse is most probable, since clients may feel that they really do not have the strength to embark on the quest. The more clients sense Presence from the therapist, the more likely they are able to take the risk to move forward.

3. Core Issues

An issue is any point, matter, or question to be disputed or decided. Whitfield (1989) says that an issue is "any conflict, concern or potential problem, whether conscious or unconscious, that is incomplete for us or needs attention or change." (P. 67) As clients become more aware via dialogue, improvisation, drawing, imaging, composing, etc. they come to understand those aspects of their life that are causing them pain. These are the core issues. Core issues start as a simple belief the child has about the world, which may be completely distorted and fictional. They begin to believe and act as if these beliefs were true. The belief can become splintered through time, generalized and even more distorted (Theme and Variations form). The "heart" of the matter lies deep within; it is the main theme on which so many distorted beliefs are then based. These are the Core Issues. In delving into these issues, the real work of therapy begins.

4. Transformation

Transformation is the act of changing form. It is the part of therapy where the client is beginning to get the "Big Picture" of how all the aspects of his life has brought him to this moment of realization and possibility for change. It is a slow and painful process, taking issues one at a time and deciding how to proceed with that issue. It is a decision-making process that in itself, transforms the client.

The process means that the client must let go of thoughts and behaviors that have kept him miserably captive, yet might be the only things that they know. To illustrate this point, I often use a song called "Love to be Loved" from the Peter Gabriel CD titled *Us* (1992). In the song he sings:

> *This old familiar craving*
> *I've been here before this way of behaving*
> *I don't know who the hell I'm saving any more*
> *Let it pass let it go let it leave*
> *From the deepest place I grieve*
> *This time I believe*
> *And I let go*
> *And I let go*

I can let go of it
Though it takes all the strength in me
And all the world can see
I'm losing such a central part of me
I can let go of it

With transformation there is a shift of thinking accompanied often by a shift of consciousness. The experiencing of the pain, working through it, and the road to making the choice of which way now to go shifts the cognitive mechanism into different modes. This shift is often aided through the music-listening experience. As people identify with music that helps in the clarification of what they feel, they can also find the applicable language to help them move forward. You can see them gain energy and momentum from music that inspires them and helps them in the nurturing of the energy for movement in their life. Jung calls this the journey of the Hero or Heroine. To overcome and be transformed takes on the implications of a heroic journey demanding courage and risk-taking. Music has the wonderful capacity to be present as an ally at this stage. The knowledge of particular music selections, which can inspire certain types of personality structures, is critically important. Yet, with individual differences, it is hard to say that certain pieces are best for everyone. You learn what inspires people musically by spending time with them musically. You learn from their improvisations, conversations, and affective responses to music.

One becomes truly transformed as one learns how to "let go" and "turn it over." Whitfield (1989) states this process best:

1. Become *aware* of our upset or concern,
2. *Experience it,* including telling our story about it,
3. Consider the *possibility* that we may have a *choice* to stop
   suffering over it, and then
4. *Let go* of it. (P. 113)

I am constantly drawn to the power of the musical experience in this stage of the recovery process. In addition to risking and talking about the story, I have found that playing the story through improvisation and composing a "sound track" to the story to be an extremely powerful means for the client. All this is done and facilitated by and in the Presence of safe others. As a music therapist, I can see the musical connections of emotion and sound, and help the client create, interpret, and find direction from the sounds.

In a seminar I attended on the *Power of the Family* by Dr. Daniel Brown, he talked about the power of the song to heal those who are survivors of any kind of abuse. Although he is not a music therapist, he has witnessed the value of this technique, which is biblically based. He cites the emotional abuse David suffered at the hands of David's father-in-law, Saul. When Saul dies, David mourns his passing with a song that celebrated his good qualities. In his book *Unlock The Power of the Family* (1994) Brown states:

> To finally be free of past abuse—especially by our parents—we must, like David, separate what they did to us from who they are (redeeming qualities). "There is nothing good about my father" is a convenient lie that justifies our desire to avenge what happened to us. The lie may sustain deep anger in our soul, but it will not heal the wounds. If you want to experience recovery, find something about your abuser to be thankful for and sing about. Thank your parents for birth, shelter, food or work ethic. Stand facing the ocean waves or in the quiet mist of the forest and sing a simple heartbreaking song of celebration about the good in your parent. And more importantly sing of all the good there might have been if your parent had properly used the covenant of being a true parent in your life. (P. 145)

5. Integration

To make whole by adding together the parts, to unify, to renew—these are the concepts of integration. The putting into practice what one is slowly learning through transforming is integration. It is an ebb and flow of meeting life's demands on a daily basis and may take years to really become assimilated into the structure of the personality. That which is learned can be unlearned, relearned, or replaced with other thoughts and behaviors.

Integration is the time when you can look at the choices that are laid out before you—the choice to move ahead in your life or stay in misery and sadness. It is a letting go of old harmful ways and integrating into the new sense of Self those realizations that were developed during Transformation.

Whitfield includes in his chapter on integration a poem by Portia Nelson. I have shared this short poem with clients and let them use it as a model to write poems of their own. We will then orchestrate the poem—either with original improvisations, compositions, or with music that the client feels adequately captures the feeling of their words. The client then reads the poem aloud to the group, and we record this for later listening by the client. As clients hear the recording of their poems with music, you can visibly see changes in their affect. I sometimes seem to see the history of their pain turning into triumph and self-realization before me. It is most powerful. Below is a poem of integration entitled *Autobiography in Five Short Chapters* by Portia Nelson.

> (1) I walk, down the street.
> There is a deep hole in the sidewalk.
> I fall in.
> I am lost . . . I am hopeless.
> It isn't my fault.
> It takes forever to find my way out.
>
> (2) I walk down the same street.
> There is a deep hole in the sidewalk.
> I pretend I don't see it.
> I fall again.
> I can't believe I am in the same place.
> But it isn't my fault.
> It still takes a long time to get out.
>
> (3) I walk down the same street.
> There is a deep hole in the sidewalk.
> I see it is there.
> I still fall in . . . it's a habit.
> My eyes are open

I know where I am.
It is *my* fault.
I get out immediately.

(4) I walk down the same street.
There is a deep hole in the sidewalk.
I walk around it.

5) I walk down another street.

6. Genesis (Spirituality)

Genesis refers to origin, a beginning. It is birth. From all that was comes all that can be. The pain, suffering, and history are not forgotten, but enable us through the stages of transformation and integration to have new choices and, in essence, a new life. As the genesis occurs, people become more aware of how their feelings and behaviors move them through time. An "Observer Self" begins to emerge. The "Observer Self," according to Deikman (1982), is that part of us that can step outside of us and see what is happening, from an objective viewpoint. It helps evaluate that which is going on and is in touch with the "True Self" as to how to respond to the whole situation. This is a very important development at this stage, for it is concrete and deals with the positive and negative aspects of behavior.

Spirituality refers to being spiritual in nature and character. It is the conversations of and with that which we call the soul. It is not of the body but of the spirit, which often finds meaning through religion. It is an experiential existence that allows for expansion of thought, awareness, and consciousness. In relationship to religion, Whitfield states that "spirituality is not organized religion, it includes it, supports it, and then transcends it" (P. 128). Religion is often thought of as a state of mind or a way of life expressing love for and trust in God. To truly experience religion, spirituality becomes an integral part of that experience. Spirituality is both a relationship with the True Self, and the relationship that exists with God.

Bradshaw (1990) calls this stage "Regeneration." He states:

Finding and reclaiming the wounded inner child is an uncovery process. In addition to developing your personal power, championing your wounded child leads to recovering his spiritual power. With his newfound spiritual power, your self-creation begins. This is your true homecoming. That which was hidden can now unfold. The urgings and signals from your deepest self can now be heard and responded to. (P. 250)

He, like Whitfield, also addresses the relationship of spirituality to religion. "The wonder child is naturally religious. He is childlike and believes in something greater than self with an unwavering faith. The wonder child's poetic soul touches the heart of being itself. Your wonder child is the part of you that possesses in a human way that power which is almost godlike: creative regeneration." (P. 257)

Spirituality is one of the most important aspects of living. Life gains meaning through the spiritual experience. The ability to be creative, spontaneous, and harmonious with self and others is heightened. For many, spirituality is at the end of a long and painful road. But when the journey is over, and this goal is reached and experienced, it becomes a true blessing.

MUSIC—THE ACTIVATING AGENT

When people are doing work in recovery, they are usually at a place in their lives where they have discovered that there is more to the existence of living than what they have been experiencing. There are signals that they have received from themselves saying, "something is wrong, life is not supposed to be this way." With this signal, they begin to look for explanations as to why it has been this way for them, as well as the possibilities of what life could become. Quite often, they are getting in touch with childhood issues, and this is a difficult and painful experience, and yet when worked through, an integrating one. They will vividly remember and express a wide range of emotions. When experiencing these emotions, music becomes the vehicle for that expression. The language of the heart is elusive, and at times they cannot find words to convey their experience. Music, sound, and often songs with lyrics become potent ways to get in touch and express feelings and/or memories that have previously escaped them, as well as helping them find a new direction.

In the group experience, music can draw the group closer together. Improvisation activities can bond or integrate the group on many different levels. The improvising and playing of music together helps the clients find their musical place in the group that might mirror or be different from their verbal place. Music can be utilized in role-playing activities between the clients as ways to re-enact childhood scenes, or to find corrective measures to the childhood scenes. Music can be the container in which emotional content can be placed. In audio or video recording of playing the emotions, the client can watch themselves—or help discover the "observer self" for an objective mode to their personal therapy. The use of video is a powerful tool in this regard. Clients not only have the sound to listen to and process, but can also see the manner in which they played the sounds, their body language. As clients go through the verbal process of telling their story, they can also compose a "soundtrack" to the story. I have done this with clients, as they often use the music to accompany drawings, mandalas, poems, prose, or written autobiographical material. This all helps in finding different emotional meanings to the experience.

With each stage of recovery that one progresses through, there can be corresponding musical activity that enables one to move through the stage. The music activities that accompany the stages can be varied. As I have already mentioned, writing songs, listening to music, improvisations, and group bonding activities are all a part of the musical process. But what do you use and when? I have found that initially, listening and imagery activities help trigger clients to get in touch with feelings. They also allow for a "safety zone" to be developed with the music therapist. There is not much of a threat to a listening activity, or so it seems. But these can be powerful ways to resonate emotional states and at the same time begin a development of trust with the clients.

The group vignette that follows is one that I use at the Stage of Integration. It is an activity that engages clients in retrospection, reaching out to others, and finding a sense of wholeness to their lives. Before I give you that vignette, I wish to offer some ideas regarding, specifically what type of music therapy activities seem to help the client through various stages.

The first stage of Survival is often one that leads a person into therapy. It must be understood that to get to the point of recovery you first have to survive (Gravitz and Bowden, 1985). Music may or may not be a major factor in this initial stage. What is a major factor is the Presence of the music therapist. Being there "ready and willing" for the client helps the client feel a sense of initial safety. He finds that on the other side of his pain is a person who is in contact with him and who will not desert him. This also paves the way for being open to different experiential music encounters. Often the resonance felt with the therapist will allow for resonance of music and the client's soul. As the soul resonates with the music, it brings to life the emotional potential of pain, courage, and healing.

Awakening or Emergent Awareness is the second stage. Music can become a true activating force in bringing to the surface, what needs to be brought to the surface. The music can "trigger" the events, memories, emotions that must be confronted and worked through. It is good to explore many types of music with the client and watch for that which causes a strong emotional reaction. The reaction does not need to be considered positive or negative; it is to be understood as a sympathetic vibration that is happening within the person to the music. The client can verbally then describe the feeling and then the therapist may help the client relate that feeling to various aspects of life. Questions such as:

> What are you experiencing (feeling) right now?
> What part of your body seems to be most tense (relaxed) right now?
> What is it about the music that has brought you to this place of feeling?
> Can you tell me what is happening to you right now?
> When have you felt this way before?
> Can you imagine a time when you might have felt this way before?
> Tell me about what you heard in the music.
> Was the music saying anything to you?
> If the music were a person, who would it be?

If the music were an emotion inside you, what would it be?
Can you draw (illustrate) what you experiencing now?

These are just a sample of some questions that can introduce the client into getting in touch with and attaching words to the experience that was stimulated by the music. The verbal content of the description is important, as it is a key to understanding why the resonance occurred. The language describing the music is the language that the music inspired within the client, which is attached to some emotional component. The component is attached to various events in the client's life. Here is the "trigger." Once it has been pulled, there is no turning back. To turn back is to deny the existence of painful reality that must be expressed and experienced overtly.

Sometimes the "trigger" is instrumental music, yet at other times it is a song that has lyrics. In many instances, I have seen clients be triggered by the combination of words and music. When this occurs, I always have the clients discuss the music and its relationship to the lyrics. I have found that without the music component, much of the effect of the lyric is lost. Simply reading the song is not enough to get things in motion. The song must have the musical element to be fully effective. The client must then also understand this "unspoken" principle (music) that enables the spoken principle (the lyric) to have such an effect upon him. If the song activates a "real" memory, which means that the song has a strong emotional attachment to a person, place, or event, then the event and the music need verbal investigation. The verbal investigation is often that which is not "owned" by the client, in that they can talk about the experience almost as if it happened to someone else. When it comes to a place of being "owned," there is a strong emotional aspect that is both painful and cathartic at the same time. Here, I then employ more improvisatory activities to enable the feeling of the emotion and the owning of it.

The triggers bring the client to the next section that is beginning to deal with Core Issues. Various music activities can help the client identify, clarify, experience, and express those aspects of thinking and being that are issues.

Improvisations that focus on or incorporate thematic elements of the issues can be used. One activity is based on the concept of the rhythm of sentences. After an appropriate warm up on the instruments, I ask the group to verbalize key core issues of the day. As they do, we put them on a blackboard for all to see and construct the issue into an appropriate sentence. Some examples are listed below:

> Don't worry 'bout me, I'm fine.
> I can't love you cause I can't love me.
> If you fail me again, I'll leave.

Each sentence has its own rhythm, but you can also organize the rhythm so that they all fit into the same sense of meter. The group plays all of them in unison to hear the power of the rhythm of each issue. A concerto format can then be organized where each member has an opportunity to "solo" on an issue. The group can also be organized into three subgroups each client playing the issue of his choice. In all these examples, an audio or video recording can be most helpful in returning to the exercise to hear, see, and analytically explore the performance from a feeling perspective, which is introduced by first conversing on the musical elements.

This group helps expend energy that is attached to issues. I have witnessed consistent affective change that occurs during exercises such as these. The clients then, in their verbal processing, have a better tone quality in their voice, pace themselves better, and are able to make positive self-statements. We then engage in positive rhythmic affirmation playing similar to that which was described above. This allows the client to leave the session with an emotional release as well as a positive emotional charge.

Another important playing activity that I do at this stage is "There are Two Sides of Me," which I adapted from one found in Carol Bitcon's *Risk-It-Express* (1989). This group centers on each client's playing for the others two sides of themselves, one on the inside, and one on the outside. The group learns the chant:

> *There are two sides of me*
> *Two sides of me*
> *One on the inside*
> *One on the outside*
> *There are two sides of me*

After the chant is taught, playing begins. A signal is given for a group member to say the chant. At the end of the chant he says, "This is my Inside (or Outside, whichever he chooses)." He then plays on his instrument this aspect of who he is. This is repeated until each person has had the opportunity to play. Once again recording the session is important so that the clients can have the opportunity to hear their musical mirror. This can also be used for Emergent Awareness, as it can energize internal feeling states that have previously been neglected or unable to be expressed.

Identifying songs for discussions that help individuals vicariously find models of expression can also be utilized here. Then going one step further is the composition of a group song. The song, similar to the improvisations of above, put into writing the core issues of the group members. The music therapist helps organize this into a coherent theme song of issues. Another song of victory, health, or integration will also be composed at some point and can become a mini-national anthem for the group. It is their song, which can begin or end groups if they wish.

Part of reaching and dealing with core issues is being able to tell "their story." In the chapter on the Jungian approach to stories and myths, you can see the correlation and validity of this approach and music therapy. Clients can present their story to the group with a narrative that is accompanied by music or improvisation that the client chooses. The music becomes a soundtrack to their story. Themes within their life can become chants, and goals they pursue can also become chants within the telling of the story; similar to a chorus of a popular song. The stories can be concrete or symbolic in nature. This process, however, takes on a completely new dimension with the addition of music. Music can add an emotional meaning to the story that often words can only imply.

The stage of Transformation is a time of turning things over to a higher power and finding forgiveness. The old story of Daedalus and Icarus is a wonderful story in this regard. I use this story with music for people in this stage, and it is also accompanied with an improvisation session that sets up the story, and then, ultimately, concludes the story. If you are not familiar with this old tale from Greek mythology let me give you a brief synopsis of the group as well as the tale, so you can get a picture of how this fits into the Transformation Stage.

The group begins with an improvisation warm up, identifying different musical instruments as different voices within the group. After a brief amount of playing (15–20 minutes), the group is asked to put the various instruments into the center of the group and sit back to listen to the story. The story begins with King Minos asking Daedalus to create a huge maze for him, which he does. When the maze is finished, King Minos refuses to let Daedalus return to his homeland with his son, Icarus. They are kept captive on the island of King Minos. Daedalus creates wings for him and his son to escape from the island. I have composed a song that is the instruction Daedalus sings to Icarus, and I teach the song to the group. The words of the song are: "Fly too low, and the sea will clog your feathers, fly too high and the sun will melt your wax." These words go unheeded by Icarus as they fly over the ocean. Here, he thinks that he is a god and tries to fly to the sun, which melts his wax, and he falls to his death. Daedalus thus loses his son because of the heat of the sun. When Daedalus reaches the shore of his homeland, he erects an altar to the god Apollo (the sun god) and worships him. It is through this act that he finds forgiveness, release, and transformation. I end the story inviting the members of the group to play on the instruments (voices of the group) that which they need to release in their lives. The subsequent playing of this on the instruments is quite powerful and cathartic. They become transformed as they play, as they grieve, and as they forgive.

Integration is making the transformation stage a part of living on a daily basis. Integration activities again often center on improvisations and compositions. It is the focusing on who the clients are becoming, more than who they once were. The main vignette of this chapter is one of integration.

The final stage is Spirituality. Here is found imaging, meditating, and personal prayer to music. These moments are some of the most powerful in the therapeutic process, as they are noetic or indescribable in character. They can be life-affirming as well as life-changing for the client. The music helps activate that which we all wish to achieve and experience, and so often like music, it is hard to describe and sometimes best left undescribed.

REFERENCES

Berne, E. (1964). Games people play: The psychology of human relationships. New York: Grove Press.

Berne, E. (1972). What do you say after you say hello? New York: Grove Press.

Bitcon, C. (1989). Risk it — express. Saint Louis: MMB Music, Inc.

Bradshaw, J. (1992). Creating love. New York: Bantam Books.

Bradshaw, J. (1990). Homecoming: Reclaiming and championing your inner child. New York: Bantam Books.

Brown, D. A. (1994). The power of the family. Nashville, TN: Sparrow Press.

Cassius, J. (1980). "Bodyscript release: How to use bioenergetics and transactional analysis." In J. Cassius (ed.), Horizons in bioenergetics: New dimensions in mind/body psychotherapy Memphis: Promethean. pp. 212–224.

Dusay, J. M., & K. M. Dusay, (1979). "Transactional analysis." In R. J. Corsini (ed.), Current psychotherapies 2nd ed. Itasca, Ill: F. E. Peacock. pp. 374–427.

Ferguson, M. (1980). The aquarian conspiracy: personal and social transformation in the 1980's. Los Angeles: Tarcher.

Gabriel, P. (1992). Us. Los Angeles: Geffin Records.

Gilliland, B. E., R. K. James & J. T. Bowman (1989). Theories and strategies in counseling and psychotherapy. 2nd ed. Englewood Cliffs, NJ: Prentice Hall, Inc.

Goldharber, G.M. & M. B. Goldharber (1976). Transactional analysis: Principles and applications. Boston: Allyn & Bacon.

Goulding, R. & M. Goulding, (1976). "Injunctions, decisions, and redecisions." Transactional Analysis Journal 6, 41–47.

Goulding, R. & M. Goulding, (1979). Changing lives through redecision therapy. New York: Brunner/Mazel.

Gravitz, H. L. & J. D. Bowden (1985). Guide to recovery: A book for adult children of alcoholics. Holmes Beach, FL: Learning Publications.

Harris, A. B. & T. A Harris. (1985). Staying OK. New York: Harper & Row, Pub.

James, M. & D. Jongeward (1971). Born to win: Transactional analysis with Gestalt experiments. Reading, MA: Addison-Wesley.

Jung, C. G. (1969). The archetypes of the collective unconscious. Princeton, NJ: Princeton University Press.

Kahler, T. & H. Capers (1974). "The miniscript." Transactional Analysis Journal 4, 26–42.

Kellogg, T. (1990). Broken toys broken dreams. Amherst, MA: BRAT Publishing.

Kurtz, R. (1990). Body centered psychotherapy: The Haikomi method. Mendocino, CA: Life Rhythm.

Miller, A. (1983). Drama of the gifted child. New York: Harper.

Nelson, P. (1977). There's a hole in my sidewalk. New York: Popular Library.

Nordoff, P. & C. Robbins (1977). Creative music therapy. New York: Harper and Row Publishers.

Nordoff, P. & C. Robbins (1985). Therapy in music for handicapped children. London: Victor Gallancz, LTD.

Whitfield, C. (1989). Healing the child within: Discovery and recovery for adult children of dysfunctional families. Deerfield Beach, FL: Health Communications, Inc.

Woolams, S. & M. Brown (1979). TA: The total handbook of transactional analysis. Englewood Cliffs, NJ: Prentice-Hall.

Chapter 10

GROUP VIGNETTE:
MUSIC THERAPY IN A RECOVERY MODEL

*Deep within you is everything that is perfect, ready to radiate
through you and out into the world. In you is all of Heaven.*

—Gifts From A Course In Miracles

THE SETTING

This clinical setting is unique, compared to many that one
might encounter in a typical practice. The clients were involved in
an intensive two-week treatment dealing with Post-Traumatic
Stress Disorder issues. The issues centered primarily on abuse that
the clients had been subjected to as children. The clients worked
with several different therapists, who were part of a team. They
were involved in many different modalities, such as art, music,
meditation, traditional group, and martial arts. There were eight
clients from various parts of the country involved in this intensive
treatment. Six were women and two were men with an average age
of 32. Since there were six in the group, I have decided to
concentrate on four of the participants, which is more reasonable to
cover for this particular vignette. The four chosen were actually a
part of two pairs, as you will see later.

I had had two previous sessions with these clients before this
final one that is described. Each session I had with them lasted for
two and a half hours and I felt that through these music sessions
we had developed a closeness and real sense of trust. We had
improvised together, worked through some old stories, shared and
improvised personal stories, and now were at a place of trying to
integrate much of what was worked through that week.

In the following descriptions I have included a "family secret"
for each client. The "family secret" is about the family's toxic
shame that as a child the client integrated into their personality.

The secret was shameful, emotionally destructive, and not discussed in any open forum.

THE CLIENTS

Mary—33-year-old white divorced woman who came from an emotionally abusive military family. Her father ruled everything, and the mother was passive aggressive. Mary has two children and has been divorced for two years after being married for ten. She feels that her childhood was stifled and that her feelings were not important. The family secret was "Don't feel anything. If you do, you are weak. Keep it to yourself."

Mark—a 39-year-old white man who is married and a father of two. He is an alcoholic. He has been in AA for eight years and relapsed a few months prior to this workshop. Precipitating factors to the relapse were being laid off and discovering his wife was having an affair with her boss. He went on a drinking spree for several days, blacked out, and ended up in a hospital. His parents were divorced when he was six, and he stayed with his mother. The father was an alcoholic and was extremely verbally abusive to him. The mother worked in a factory and after the divorce became very promiscuous. He was the only child. The family secret— Daddy's a drunk, Mommy sleeps around.

Angie—a 45-year-old white woman who has been divorced twice and has no children. Both relationships were physically and emotionally abusive. She is a secretary at a law firm. Her father molested her from the age of 6 till she was 8. She told her mother when she was older, but her mother did not believe her and disowned her. Her father denied the abuse also. The family secret—dad is having sex with me, and if I tell, he won't love me anymore.

Jan—A 28-year-old unmarried college graduate with a degree in business. Her parents divorced when she was 4 and her sister was 2. Her mother's boyfriend molested her from the age of 10 till 11. When her mother found out she became very angry, broke up with the boyfriend but ceased to have a close relationship with Jan. Family secret—I stole Mommy's boyfriend and now she hates me.

THE SET UP

The session that follows is one that I do as part of the Integration stage. I have given this the title of "In Your Eyes," as it deals with looking at ourselves as an integrating whole and drawing energy from this synthesis. This process occurs through contact with other group members, imagery, improvisation, and the looking at a small mirror—mainly at your own eyes—while listening to a selected piece of music.

I have devised this group almost as one would compose a piece of music. I have attempted to take the clients through various stages of group and individual work, much as a composer might want to take an audience through different emotions by varying themes, harmonies, and tonal centers. This group moves from the whole group doing a group activity, to dyads, to individual time, back to dyads, and ending with group work again. This progression serves many functions. First, there is an establishment of group trust through the first activity. At times, the trust appears to be fragile, and indeed, often is. The movement into improvisation helps bind the group rhythmically, and the real groundwork of group trust is laid. From this, they move into dyads and improvise on slit drums—trust is now occurring on a one-on-one level. They then do some individual work through both imagery and also actual viewing of their eyes and face through small hand mirrors that are provided for them. This activity helps them gain trust in themselves. As they listen to the song, read the lyrics, and look into the mirror, the integration occurs. This is the center and apex of the whole activity. I have seen a wide range of affective responses happen at this stage of the group. Sometimes, there are tears, and sometimes there are looks of contentment and release. After this, they start the process of coming back to the group first through dyad work and then finally in a group improvisation. Much like a composition that has a recapitulation, the group comes back more grounded, trusting, and self-reliant as a group because of the individual processes that they had gone through.

This is an integration group primarily because of what happens for each individual as well as for the group. I have found that clients feel much more in touch with themselves and grounded when this activity is over. The group also becomes much more integrated as a group. As the individuals make progress toward their own integration they come to rely on and support others in a more meaningful way.

I have prepared for each client a stapled handout consisting of eight pages. This handout is a series of instructions and cues for the clients to follow. On page 6 is the song "In Your Eyes" (1992) by Peter Gabriel. The song's recurrent chorus is:

> *In your eyes—the light the heat*
> *In your eyes—I am complete*
> *In your eyes—I see the doorway to a thousand churches*
> *In your eyes—the resolution of all the fruitless searches*
> *Oh, I see the light and the heat*
> *In your eyes—oh, I want to be that complete*
> *I want to touch the light the heat I see in your eyes*
> *In your eyes—In your eyes—*

When the clients hear the chorus, many of them are looking into a small mirror that is provided for them. I have found that this experience has been a vital part of the integration process for many clients.

Another important line that many clients have identified with is:

> *All my instincts, they return*
> *And the grand facade, so soon will burn*
> *Without a noise, without my pride, I reach out from the*
> *inside.*

In this line, clients begin to identify instinctual qualities they may have forgotten they had or did not know existed. Again, with the final line, an integrative experience occurs for the clients as they look into the mirror and see themselves reaching out through their own eyes from the inside of their being.

The following is the content of the handout.

Cover Page:
There will be no talking for the remainder of the group
   experience.
If you do not understand a direction, trust your instincts.
As you are reading this, you will hear a chime. This chime is
   your cue to change activities or to turn a page and return to
   this handout.
When you are finished reading this, make eye contact with
   your leader. When everyone has done this, you will hear
   the chime. At that point turn the page.

Page 2:
In a sitting position make a group circle around the crystal
   toning bowl.
(It is optional to hold hands with your neighbor.)
Listen to the tone of the bowl.
Experience the tone, and if you wish, hum along with it.
As you hum, close your eyes and continue humming until you
   hear the tone, at which point you will slowly bring your
   humming to an end and open your eyes.
After the tone—turn the page.

Page 3:
In front of you are percussion instruments and paddle drums.
Find an instrument and begin playing. Try to create a group
   sound.
If you can't find the rhythm, listen for the beat of your leader.
When you hear the tone, gradually bring the group sound to a
   conclusion.
After you hear the tone—turn the page.

Page 4:
Break up into pairs
Go play together on a slit drum—listen to each others' rhythm
   and try to get a pattern together.
When you hear the tone, gradually bring your playing to a
   conclusion.
Wait till all have stopped playing.
After the tone—turn the page.

Page 5:
Find a comfortable place in the room to lie down.
Get as relaxed as possible.
As you close your eyes, imagine looking at yourself in the
   mirror.

See yourself as a child, see yourself as you are today, and as
  you may look in the future.
There will be music in the background.
Do this until you have heard the tone.
After the tone—make eye contact with your leader.
At his signal—turn the page.

Page 6:
As the music begins, if you wish, follow the lyrics given to
  you, glance in the mirror provided for you from time to
  time.
When the song is over, take a few moments for yourself.
When you hear the tone, turn the page.

Page 7:
Find your partner from before. Play together with any of the
  instruments you wish.
When you hear the tone, gradually find a conclusion to your
  playing.
Return to the circle, and turn the page.

Page 8:
Find any instrument, and begin to play as a group.
When you hear the tone, gradually find a conclusion to the
  improvisation.
Put your instrument down.

The room in which this group took place was large with
enough space to easily fit more than what was included in this
group. There were overstuffed pillows, on which the clients could
sit or lie. I had stacked the chairs in the corner, opting for sitting on
the pillows and carpeted floor. I had arranged the room prior to the
entrance of the clients. In the center was the 14-inch quartz crystal
toning bowl. Around it were five African slit drums, each having
four mallets resting on top. Moving out away from the slit drums
were the following percussion instruments arranged also in a circle
with the crystal bowl being the center: ten paddle drums (8-, 10-,
and 12-inch sizes), tambourine, two wood blocks, one pair of rattle
sticks (these are long tubes with BB's in them and sound similar to
maracas), one cabassa, one two-toned wood block, one African
agogo, two egg shakers (plastic eggs that are filled with BB's and
sound similar to maracas), one pair of maracas, and three hand

drums (10, 12, and 14 inch sizes). Circling the outside of the instruments were the large pillows for the clients.

Instead of using the overhead fluorescent lights, I brought in two table lamps. I feel that the lamp lighting is more conducive to the session than the overheads. There seems to be a softer quality of light that helps the clients feel more at ease and open to the musical activity. Clients have often remarked to me about the Presence of the room when they walk in. The lighting and layout of the instruments have an easy appeal to the visual sense. This attractiveness appears to enable a feeling state that the client finds comfortable and safe. There again is a sense for them that something different is about to happen in music therapy, and indeed, something different was about to happen.

THE SESSION

The Beginning—Warm up

The clients come into the room, slowly some talking to one another and others coming in by themselves. As they enter, I greet each one by name. I decide not to have music playing as they come in today. With this particular integration group and this part of their treatment, I prefer no entry music. I feel that what is to come in the group should not have a musical prelude.

The layout of the room and the novelty of the slit drums catch everyone's attention as they gather on the pillows around the instruments. The atmosphere appears warm and relaxed as the clients settle in.

I address all the clients and get some basic information as to how things have been going since the last time I had contact with them. There is some discussion regarding the new instruments they see—mainly the slit drums. I have them listen to the bowl and do some deep breathing exercises to help them prepare for the group.

We then have a brief warm up period of exploring different groups of instruments and playing together. First, they play the paddle drums, then, various percussion instruments, and finally the slit drums. This group readily finds a group beat and integrates well together. The general mood is elevated as they play.

I help bring the improvisation to a close. I tell them a brief overview of the group so that they have some idea as to what is going to happen. I describe to them that this will be a music therapy experience. Through this experience, there should be no verbal discussion or questions as the handouts are self-explanatory. I also demonstrate for them the sound of the chime that will be listened for as a cue throughout the activity. The chime is a pair of hand cymbals from India. Before I hand out the packets, I ask if there are any questions, and there are none. I proceed with handing out the packets.

As I said before, this vignette will focus on four clients and their response and interaction through the group. All four are sitting next to each other. They are arranged as follows: Jan, Mary, Angie, then Mark. As they finish the first page of instructions, they all make eye contact with me.

Middle

The group turns to the second page after hearing the chime where they are to listen to the quartz bowl and hum and join hands if they wish. The group readily joins hands, but is hesitant at first to hum. I have found that when groups are asked to explore with their voice without much warm up or work with the voice, they are usually hesitant to use it in an expressive manner. Even though humming seems to be a safe activity, this group is having trouble feeling comfortable with their voices. This is also something typical of abuse or post traumatic stress patients. Finding an expressive use of the vocal mechanism seems to be threatening and initially difficult to do. After about a minute, some members of the group begin to hum, attempting to match the pitch of bowl. I can discern that Jan, Angie, and Mary are humming slightly and near pitch. Mark's hum is out of tune with the bowl, and he is searching to match the pitch but is unable to and fades out. All the clients have also closed their eyes as requested in the instructions. The activity of closing the eyes is another threatening thing for these clients, as well as for many others. There must be a sense of trust between the group and the therapist for this to happen, as clients become very vulnerable when their eyes are closed. If this had been the first time asking them to close their eyes, I would have said something like, "If you are comfortable with it, you can close your eyes, if you don't want to, that's OK. Sometimes, when we close our eyes, it can enhance the experience we are involved in." This instruction, when given in a calm, directed, and well paced voice can be the anchor for the client who has been wanting to trust someone, and has been working on the trust issue with you or others throughout treatment.

During this time, I feel that there is a different type of trust that is beginning to occur within the group. They are all, at some level, engaging in an activity that is new to them. They are experiencing this as a group unit. They are hearing the imperfections of their voices, the touch of their neighbor's hand, and, because their eyes are closed, a heightening of the experience. The experience of the second page comes to an end with the sounding of the chime.

The third page is an improvisation page. Mary immediately picks up a paddle drum and establishes a group beat. The beat is strong and solid. As she is doing this, other members are finding instruments and joining in. As I watch Mary play, I can't help but be struck at the regiment of the beat—similar to a military unwavering cadence. I reflect on her issues of her militaristic father and abusive past. She continues a driving beat with minimal body movement.

Jan chose an agogo and initially experimented within the beat. She then found a pattern that she then kept throughout this improvisation. The pattern was not a dominating sound, even though she had a very loud instrument—she seemed to be wanting to blend in with the group. Rather than being lost in the sound, it sounded as if she was more involved in finding safety within the beat and the group.

Mark chose two rattle-stick shakers. His sound seemed very lost in the background—introspective in a way. His body language was closed, and he seemed to be going inside himself, which appears different from a regressive movement. His sound was fitting in with the group, but definitely in a background manner.

Angie chose the tambourine. She closed her eyes and seemed to listen to the sounds around her. She was sitting erect and moving her body with the beat. She played with a good sense of energy and seemed to be complimenting Mary's beat. With this, she seemed to be trying to make some type of musical contact. Musical contact can be achieved without eye contact, yet, when members do acknowledge each other with their eyes and body, the musical contact seems more complete. This type of non-body music contact is often initially safer for group members, since they only need to rely on the sense of hearing rather than on eye contact, with is often more threatening.

After a few minutes, there seems to be a good sense of group rhythmic interaction. The group, however, is doing this on a nonvisual level. Most group members are not looking at others. They are either playing with their eyes closed or looking at their instruments. I sound the chime. The group comes to a rather quick and awkward close. They turn the page to see the instructions on page four.

On page four of the instructions, they break into pairs sharing a slit drum for each pair. Mary and Jan are in one pair, and Angie and Mark are in another. Mary again establishes a strong beat on the slit drum and is obviously the dominant force. Jan does not really play with Mary, but instead is trying to fit a beat in between the beats of Mary. It appears and sounds awkward. Her attempts at fitting in are awkward and are not really working well. The dominance of Mary—again an projection of her father's personality, is overwhelming the pair. Other than outright fighting for the beat—or just copying it, Jan is trying to fit in. The ego strength of Jan is not at a place where it can truly match the power of Mary. This also plays into the life pattern of how Jan has dealt with her past and the world.

Angie and Mark, on the other hand, are playing well together. They are interacting rhythmically on their slit drum. Their body language is less rigid but there is no eye contact. I play the tone and the group again comes to a rather abrupt halt. They return to their outlines and turn to page five.

Page five instructs the individuals of the group to become comfortable, close their eyes, and as they listen to music imagine that they are looking in the mirror. In this image, they are to see themselves as they looked as a child, as they are today, and as they might look in the future. I am improvising on the guitar for this experience. I am playing a slow almost arhythmic improvisation that starts with a single line and then slowly adds harmonic structure. This lasts about four to five minutes. I close the improvisation by ending with the single line again. I observe that there are no remarkable changes at this time. I sound the chime that indicates that it is time to turn the page and read the next instruction.

Page six is the focal point for this activity. It is here that each member receives a little hand-held mirror. They are instructed to listen to the song "In Your Eyes" by Peter Gabriel. As they listen, they are to look in the mirror at their eyes from time to time.

As the music begins, Mary sits up and immediately begins to move her upper body to beat. Her eyes are closed as she listens. With each chorus of the song, she opens her eyes and looks in the mirror. Her body movement at this time diminishes, but returns after each chorus

Jan is lying on her stomach reading the words. She is intermittently taking long looks into the mirror.

Angie lies on her back holding the words above her in one hand, and the mirror in the other. She also is taking long looks in the mirror throughout the song. At the end of the song, she puts down the words and the mirror and closes her eyes.

Mark initially takes a few quick looks in the mirror, and then doesn't look into it for much of the song. During the last chorus, he puts the words down, lies on his back, and looks into the mirror for the remainder of the song.

The final instructions on page six allow for a few moments of silence so that the group can simply experience what they are feeling. Jan, Mary, Mark, and Angie all are lying now on their backs with their eyes closed. I sound the chime—they pick up their booklet and turn to page seven.

Page seven asks the group members to pair up with the person they were with before. They are to choose any of the instruments and play together. Mark and Angie choose a large paddle drum. They both begin to play a strong beat in unison. The sound is so strong that it is dominant over the group sound, and in fact most of the group is starting to play within it. Mark and Angie begin to make eye contact with each other and also begin to smile. The image that comes to mind for me as I watch them is of two grownups being children. They are playing together, complimenting each other's rhythm and acknowledging each other with their eyes.

Jan and Mary return to the slit drum that they were playing before. Mary seems less domineering in her beat. Jan is initially falling into the pattern she was in earlier where she is trying to fit her beat in between those of Mary. This is short-lived, however, as she then starts to play right along with Mary. They soon begin to play the same rhythm in unison, and at this point they look at each other and start to laugh.

It seems as if most of the group is making more eye contact and interacting on more than a musical level at this point. Mark and Angie have established a beat in the background that most of the group has now conformed to. I sound the chime that indicates to the group to return to a group circle and to develop a group improvisation. We are now on the final page of the booklet.

I notice immediately that Mary does not return to the drum that she used in the first group improvisation so strongly. She instead chooses the cabassa. While she is still forceful in her playing, it is not dominating the beat but instead integrating within the group beat. This seems to be a carry over from the previous activity.

Jan returns to the agogo she played earlier. Her rhythms are much freer and creative within the beat. Her body is moving and is not as rigid. She begins to make eye contact around the room and connects with another group member across from her. They begin to unify on the same rhythmic pattern. They begin to smile and make good eye contact as they play.

Angie returns to the tambourine. She too is more playful and creative with her rhythm. She is making eye contact around the room and also moving her body to the beat.

Mark takes up the rattle sticks that he was playing earlier. His body is more upright than it was earlier. He is playing with the sticks out in front of him, forcefully and also freely within the beat. He initially plays with his eyes closed. After a short period of time, he opens his eyes and begins to look around the room. He connects with another member across from him who is playing the egg shakers. They, like some of the other members, begin to play the same rhythmic pattern in unison. After going through the pattern a few times, they smile.

The improvisation as a whole is very unified and energetic. There is more of a sense of group beat and balance that is markedly different from the group improvisation at the beginning of the activity. Throughout the group, there is more eye contact, rhythmic imitation and unison, and body movement within the beat. By the end of the improvisation, all the members have smiled at least one time during this last activity. All members have made eye contact with at least one other member.

I play the chime, and for the first time in the activity, there is a gradual fading out of the instruments. The last instruments to be playing are the egg shakers and Mark on the rattle sticks. They fade out with slow shaking.

Ron	OK . . . put your instruments down . . . take a few deep breaths . . . and get in touch with what you are feeling and experiencing right now.

I do this because it seems that everyone is in a very good place both physically and emotionally. It is important to have everyone become aware of these good sensations. They can use these as anchors for another time, as well as confirming the important fact that they are allowed to feel this way.

Ron	If you wish, close your eyes as you breathe and let each breath bring a new sense of life into you. (I allow for about a minute to pass.) You all have done very well in following the directions on the page, as well as not speaking throughout the session. But now it's time to talk just a little bit before we go tonight. Think of the last improvisation that you all just did together—if you could give it a title, what would it be?
Jan	Celebration!
Mary	Freedom . . . totally freeing . . . yeah—freedom.
Angie	Trust.
Robert	Spiritual play.
Ron	So it seems like, overall, the last improvisation was a good experience for you. Reflect for a moment on the

	whole activity. Is there any thing you would like to mention? How certain parts were for you?

Jan The whole thing was so cool . . . I felt a real sense of trust and being together that is different from the other groups that we are in. This feeling is hard for me to describe . . . just a warmth and trust.

Ron I noticed that when you were playing with Mary on the slit drums, your playing with her changed from the first time to the second—did you notice that?

Jan Kind of—the second definitely felt better.

Ron In the first you looked frustrated—you were trying to play around her beats and rhythm—as if you were trying to "fit in." What do you think about that?

Jan Oh my God!—That's exactly what we were talking about today in my small group—that I try to conform to what other people want me to be—maybe because I have had no idea of who I was.

Ron So what happened the second time?

Jan I got frustrated and said "the hell with it" and just started playing whatever I felt.

Ron What happened next?

Jan Let me think—(she smiles)—I was playing and it sounded good with Mary—we were together

Ron Together . . . and how did that happen again?

Jan I just played . . . I followed my instincts?

Ron Followed your instincts?

Jan Yeah . . . you know what I mean . . .

Ron Do I? (Pause.) So you followed your instincts, and that felt . . . ?

Jan Good—no great!

Ron You called the last improvisation "Celebration." Why?

Jan Because it all just kind of came together and sounded so uplifting—as if we were celebrating something.

Ron And what can you celebrate today?

Jan That I could play—connect—trust—and I could be myself—no sense of expectations from others—I could just be.

Ron To just **BE**, is important, and it is important to understand

	that you just experienced that. This is good . . . someone else?
Mary	Well, that's my favorite song . . . and, well, I feel totally liberated! I feel free to be who I am, and not really care about what others might think. I enjoyed the integration of the whole group. I found that looking into my eyes to be very powerful. I saw a clarity in them—an innocence—softness—things that I usually don't see in myself. I want to thank you for this group.
Ron	You're welcome . . . So it was a sense of freedom?
Mary	Yeah . . . liberated—I feel like I've been trapped by so much through all my life—and now, at this moment, I feel free.

I am impressed when musical experiences such as these enable the clients to find, if for even a few moments, strong positive feelings that they may have not felt for a long time if ever. These feelings can also be called upon during treatment to give clients hope when they feel like giving up.

Ron	(I nod and smile at Mary.)
Angie	I felt a spiritual sense of trust among this group . . . and that means so much to me. I never feel like I can trust people, and I have been learning to trust this group of people this week, but tonight, it was really there, it was genuine.
Ron	Why do you think that happened?
Angie	Playing together with others, especially Mark, just seemed to bind us together in a way that we haven't been yet. We found rhythms together, smiled at one another . . . this is the first time this week where I have seen people smile. I have seen them get angry, sad, be depressed . . . and tonight I saw some smile . . . that was great.

This response from Angie is one that I have heard on many occasions. Not only does it occur with this particular group activity, but very often when the group gets comfortable playing with one another and seemingly communicating with their instruments. The non-verbal bond that happens when people play music with one another is powerful and longlasting. This is part of the unique power that music has for healing; it makes music therapy special.

Mark	Since Angie said the word "spiritual," I want to pick up on that. But before I do, I want to thank you, Ron, for this group, it has meant a lot to me. (Mark takes a long, deep breath and starts his words slowly, and appears to be searching for the right things to say to get his point across.) I feel like something very spiritual happened to me through this session. I had forgotten what it was like to be a child. As I have grown older, I have struggled with being an adult . . . and I think it is because the foundation of being a child was missing from my life experience. I missed out on so much of my childhood . . . when life was so supposed to be happy and carefree, it was hell for me. And now I am struggling with how to have integrity, spirituality, and how to be a man. But through this group, I have come to an important realization that we have been talking about all week, and that is that I have this little boy inside me—and I allowed that little boy to come out and play—especially when Angie and I were playing on the drum. So . . . I think if I can allow that little boy to play through this adult body . . . I can maybe fill in some of the missing foundations in my life.
Ron	Those are very powerful words and realizations.
Mark	Yeah . . .
Ron	Mark, I saw that you initially didn't look much in the mirror during the song.
Mark	You know, that was the hardest part of this group for me. At first, I was really scared to look in the mirror. I first looked at my eyes and really didn't like what I saw. Then, something happened as I was listening to the words "I am complete." I looked in the mirror, and for the first time in a long, time, I found some trust in my own eyes. I started

to see things in them that I have never seen before—I was no longer afraid.

Ron   Afraid?

Mark   Afraid of looking at myself in the eyes and only seeing a complete and total failure. I am not going to be that any more.

Ron   (I nod to Mark.) I believe that . . . You really do have a different look about you than earlier in the group. It is a good look, and it really becomes you.

Often the affect of people will change through the group. You can see their eyes have more clarity and a sense of optimism. They hold their body in a more confident position. I have seen actual skin color come back to those who were very pale. A face might look more calm and relaxed at the end of a group. I feel that it is very important to let the person know that this outward appearance of healthy change is noticeable. It can be extremely reinforcing and powerful.

End

Ron   We will end tonight's group as we have ended our groups in the past. (I hold and sound the harmony ball.) As we pass this around, I invite you to share with the group what you will remember from this evening. (I roll the ball to Jan.)

Jan   This was really cool . . . I will remember that I can be me, and that's OK. (She rolls the ball to Mary.)

Mary   Like I said before, this group was liberating for me. I felt free, not judged by others . . . and I will remember my favorite song being played, and it was about me. (She rolls the ball to Angie.)

Angie   I have found that I can trust others, This is so important for me—and I will always remember this feeling. Thank you. (She rolls the ball to Mark.)

Mark   I will allow myself to play in this adult body. I will not forget that there is a little boy inside who wants to play .. and it is OK for him to play.

FINAL THOUGHTS

The other four clients also shared the fact that they had gone through a positive experience. Their comments centered on the feelings of becoming whole and more self-assured. They found that they also felt more connected with other group members.

The second male client, Jim, shared with the group that throughout the song he was thinking about his grandfather who died the year before. He said he, like Mark, was initially afraid to look in the mirror. When he really started looking in his eyes, his eyes were not his own, but those of his grandfather. He found comfort in looking at his eyes and said that he realized that his grandfather, although dead, would always be inside of him.

Using music is a valuable aid to the process of integration in this recovery model. Integration is putting the parts of oneself together and feeling a sense of renewal. This is accomplished in this particular music activity. It occurred not only on an individual basis, but also the group left the session feeling more integrated, and refreshed.

Overall, music sessions can be an integral part of the recovery model. Music helps the clients move through the various stages in a creative way, often bringing them to a more spiritual place in their lives.

Chapter 11

WORDS AND MUSIC

Our life is what our thoughts make it.

—Marcus Aurelius (2nd c.)

One of the things I have noticed in working with clients is that many of them have a difficult time thinking clearly. Often I will hear clients say things such as, "I am so confused, all my thoughts are jumbled," or "If I could only clear my head, I would know what to do." Their words are reflecting the inability to figure things out, to make sense of what is going on inside. They are not sure of what they are feeling, and they are lost. This confusion even further disrupts the search for equilibrium in their lives. In times like this, music, and more specifically songs, can actually help in organizing, filtering, and acting upon thoughts, clarifying feelings, and providing direction. They find resonance in the words, sympathetic vibration in the sounds, and with the help of the music therapist, they learn how to use the connection of this experience (Lippin, 1983). Additionally, through the group process of looking at lyrics and music, they can learn new and better coping strategies, and receive validation for their feelings (Freed, 1987).

THE MIRROR

The re-establishment of meaning in a chaotic thought system is the way to heal it. It is but your thoughts that bring you fear, and your deliverance depends on you. What I see reflects a process of my mind, which starts with the idea of what I want. I can be hurt by nothing but my thoughts.

—Gifts From A Course In Miracles

Almost without exception, when a group of clients hear a collection of songs that are in some way related to their treatment, many of the clients will respond with the following statements:
"That's exactly how I feel."

"I feel like they are writing about me."
"I couldn't have said it any better, it is exactly where I am at."
"This one line describes what I feel perfectly."

The list is but a brief summary of typical responses. What they all have in common is the personal link of the lyrics/music being an accurate descriptor of their current level of functioning, previous level of functioning, or future goal. Staff members have often mentioned that when clients choose songs to listen to, they are often related to their diagnoses (Metzger, 1986).

What I found to be most fascinating is that the impact of written words is strongest when accompanied by music. When the lyrics are simply read from a sheet of paper, almost like poetry, they are not nearly as effective as when they are heard to music and combined with the visual stimulus of reading the lyrics as they are sung. I feel that this is probably because of the way the brain is processing information. If one just reads the words, the visual channel is basically the only channel from which the information is being processed. When music is accompanying the words, the overall stimuli are greater. The client is now using visual as well as auditory stimuli. Emotional parts of the brain are more easily engaged through the presentation of the words with music.

One interesting reaction often happens. When certain songs that are familiar to clients are played, the clients may be surprised by the fact they "never listened to the song quite like this before." Or they may say, "I never really understood what the song was saying." This revelation for clients may be the result of a few factors. First, they are in an emotional place at this point in time where the song has a different emotional effect on them than in previous hearings. Even if it was "learned" to stimulate a different emotional response, it now has a different overall effect. Second, the combined stimuli of reading and listening seems to be processed differently, which allows for a wider possibility of emotional stimulation. I have had many clients attest to this phenomenon. The song is thus heard almost as though it were "new" because of the combined stimuli. And third, in their previous listening and learning of the familiar song, they may have learned it as if by rote, not really processing it to understand the meaning.

Whatever the reason, familiar songs can bring about a variety of emotional responses from the client. Due to the preceding factors, the responses may be quite different from those the therapist might expect. The response is the first step in understanding the clients' thinking and feeling state. Their belief system becomes more evident as they then discuss their reactions to the lyrics and music.

I will often ask clients to critique whether or not the music is actually appropriate for the lyrics—whether it adds or subtracts from the meaning of the words. I have found that clients can be quite expressive and insightful when speaking of music as an accompaniment to lyrics. Their critiques come from a feeling base that is then cognitively expressed. Through their discussion of the music, they are presenting cues to their current emotional and/or cognitive state. In the first chapter, I spoke of how to watch for this. The verbal descriptors of the music describe what is going on in their life. The music therapist can then help to integrate the verbalizations, so that the client can gain additional meaning and insight.

The process of deciding what songs to use is based upon the needs and issues of the group. There tend to be "universal" issues that touch most clients. Some of these universal issues are

Friendship	Betrayal	Support
Independence	Relationship	Dependency
Finding Oneself	Life Changes	Divorce
Separation	Finance	Materialism
Spirituality	Gender Issues	Emotions
Reaching Out	Goals	Decision Making
Morality	Chemical Dependency	

Within these "universal" issues, clients have their own specific story. Their story can find resonance in the songs they listen to. From this point, clients are oftentimes given the means to tell, discuss, find meaning, and answers for their story. They will often have the "light bulb" go on above their head and make transitions from looking back to looking ahead.

Finding songs for this style of group can be both structured and, at times, serendipitous. The beginning process is, for me, usually by chance. I hear a song and from my own projections feel that it might fit into one of the "universal" categories. Then a structured process begins a search for one to two other songs that have a similar theme, but might approach the subject matter differently. Once the songs are found, I look at them from the perspective of the therapist presenting the songs to the client, and then, as the client having the songs presented.

From the therapist's perspective, I consider:

1. The Theme and what group it might be appropriate for.
2. The order of the songs presented—which is based upon how the overall material flows from one song to another.
3. What should be learned from each song and how this can be tied into the overall group.
4. What can clients take with them from this experience to help them in their overall treatment process.

In attempting to listen from the clients' perspective, I listen to the music as if I were hearing it for the first time. I also listen as if I had directions as to what to listen for. I then ask these questions: "Can I hear it in a way the client might hear it? Does it keep my attention? Is it something that I might be able to relate to or find familiar to current musical taste?"

A session I call "Decision Making" has been quite successful for me and developed through the process that I have just described. This particular intervention uses three songs. I start with "Meeting Across the River" (1975) by Bruce Springsteen. The song, from my perspective, has two concepts regarding *aspects* of the decision-making process. One aspect is control. You are in control of your own decisions—unless you decide to give up the control. Once control is given up, however, it is difficult to recover. The second concept is that as you make a decision, you usually rely on past experience to help in making the decision. This first song thus serves as a starting point in this process.

The second song is "Fast Car" (1988) by Tracy Chapman. The first song is concerned with one basic decision and how it might effect a current situation. "Fast Car" deals with decisions that affect a person's entire life. In the process of making the decisions, we also see in this song a destructive behavioral pattern that has been passed down through a generation, a pattern that the singer then decides to change. The clients learn several things from this song.

First, they come understand that something is wrong. The feelings that they are experiencing have become a strong indicator of this. Second, they learn that to break a destructive pattern they are involved in they must acknowledge that it exists. You can't work on changing something that you don't own as your behavior or thought process. Third, they must decide to do something about it. This can be seeking treatment, or support. If they are already in treatment, then it might be looking at ways to change aspects of their lives in order to live a more effective and fuller existence.

Another point that will often come out of the song, is that unless you go through this process of *Feelings, Insight, and Change,* you will end up in the same destructive patterns and relationships, even if you change geographical locations. As part of the discussion, the first song is linked with the second by mentioning the aspects of control in the whole story. In discussing the music that accompanies the second song, there is a repetitive accompaniment figure that goes with the verses. This is discussed in relation to the repetitive behavior patterns in life. In contrast to the verses, the chorus initiates a change of rhythmic feel and instrumentation. The clients discuss the reason why this occurs as it is in relationship to a break in the behavior pattern of the singer.

"Eye of the Hurricane" (1989) by David Wilcox is an excellent song in which to start bringing the session to a close. This song is about a woman who rides a motorcycle called a "Hurricane." She, like the woman in the previous song, has made certain choices (decisions) in her life, all which have had a lasting imprint. The final choice is putting herself in such danger that she loses her life. Other choices she has made include giving up on her dream and not allowing herself to experience emotional pain. These are discovered through the lyrics by the presentation of the question to the group, "There are three critical decisions that are made in this song—try to figure out what they are."

The main aspects of the three songs are then brought together to present a challenge to the group. I take them through a simplified relaxation exercise and ask them to reflect on the entire session. I then ask them to think of one decision that they are currently working on or in need of making. Then, they imagine themselves making the decision, and what the outcome would be. They are asked to try to feel the emotional sensation of making the decision. The session ends with each member sharing with the group the decision he or she imaged.

I have used this method of putting three to four songs together with a common theme with success. Clients find that they will often relate to the themes, lyrics, and music in a very personal manner. Presenting the songs is almost a "class like" learning situation, the clients feel they are learning something from the session, which differs from a typical group therapy approach, that often begins with "What are you feeling today?"

NEUROLINGUISTIC PROGRAMMING

Bandler and Grinder (1975) developed a technique called Neurolinguistic Programming (NLP), and I have used this in many different types of settings. I wish to include a bit about their theory here since this chapter is concerned with words, and in the vignette that follows I draw from this approach.

The philosophy is based upon a communication theory whereby people process information based upon their five sensory channels. These channels are called *Representational* systems and contain the following: visual (sight), auditory (hearing), kinesthetic (feeling), olfactory (smell), and gustatory (taste). The basic premise of the theory is that people map their inner experiences, and then through the process of communication, they give you the keys to their map. One of the keys is in the form of what words, specifically verbs-or predicates they use to describe their map.

In therapy sessions, I have found that most people use words from the visual, auditory, or kinesthetic representational systems. For example, a client says, "I can't *see* my way out of this." My reply might be, "It's hard to get a picture of where to go?" I respond to the verb *see* with the word *picture*, which is part of the

visual representational system. An auditory example would be—
the client says "I keep *telling* myself—I can do it." My response
might be "I *hear* that in your words." If the client says "I *feel* that
there's no good answer." I might respond, "Well, maybe we should
work on getting a *handle* on little stressors first." If you would
refer back to Chapter 4 and review the list of lead-in phrases by
Hammond, Hepworth and Smith (1978), you can find more
examples of this.

In all of these examples, I am responding to verbal cues by
using predicates within the identified representational systems. By
doing this, I am consciously becoming aware of the frame of
reference for the client and the keys to their internal map. I am also
responding to nonverbal clues, breathing, and overall body
language. The result is that a *synchrony* develops, and clients begin
to sense that the therapist is *in tune* with their experience. This is
known as *pacing*, where I am sensing and responding to the inner
experiences of the client—much like empathy. From this, rapport
is established and trust can be built.

The NLP technique, however, is more than matching
predicates. Bandler and Grinder offer in-depth techniques within
this theory that are far too numerous to mention here. But a sketch
of this technique for this vignette is important, even at a basic
level. Through this technique, the therapist learns to consider the
following: how to listen to a client; how to respond to a client; and
how to be cognitively aware of the whole interaction that will
ultimately lead to a greater sense of Presence, which the client will
perceive.

STAGES OF TREATMENT

When I was a younger therapist, and in my first "real" full-time
music therapy job, I learned something that intrigued me from a
treatment team review of a client. The psychiatrist began talking
about stages of emotional progression for adolescents as they are
treated in an inpatient psychiatric facility. Following the treatment
review, I began to take note of this phenomenon, and observed, for
the most part, that the psychiatrist had some interesting and good

insights regarding this progression. I expanded on this basic concept and began to use it in my therapeutic approach.

Knowing the progression of a client through treatment is relevant for the therapist. By clarifying stages that clients progress through as they are "interned" in the psychiatric hospital system, the therapist can:

1. Plan appropriate sessions for the stage the client is in.
2. Be more cognizant of the type of information that the client is willing or able to share within the current stage.
3. Help clients, through various types of groups, to understand what stage they are currently going through and perhaps find a strategy to move forward.

The music therapy group that is to follow is based upon the premise that clients go through developmental stages of treatment. My thoughts on this have altered slightly through the years, but I have come to believe that most clients who are in a short-term facility go through these stages. These stages are also based on the assumption that the client is going to move positively through the treatment process.

The stages of treatment are as follows:

1. *Pre-treatment or crisis*: In this stage, clients have not yet entered a treatment program. They may, however, be in outpatient therapy. There is a precipitating crisis. The client moves into a state where he feels, his family feels, or society deems necessary, that he enter a full clinical program.

2. *Early*: The client is introduced to the unit and usually a structured way of living each day. He is meeting new peers, therapists, nurses, etc. He is getting involved in various therapeutic modalities, many of which have not been encountered before. There is usually some level of apprehension, anxiety, and confusion. The client might not be actively working on specific issues at this time, unless they are directly related to the precipitating crisis. He may be unwilling to verbalize much in a group structure or be hyper verbal regarding the crisis. He may be unwilling to come to the group session, especially if he has never

had music therapy before. To alleviate some of the music therapy phobia, it is good to make a positive contact with the client before the first session ever occurs. Let him know who you are and what you do. I have a few sayings that I will think of from time to time when working with a client in this stage. One is "Gentler is better." Another is based on the saying "Treat others as you would like to be treated." In other words, imagine from time to time being in a place like the psychiatric unit for the first time. How would you perceive the music therapist?

3. *Middle*: In this time period the client moves from the emotional, confusing early stage, to a more introspective but possibly turbulent period. The client begins to undergo an emotional catharsis, and through this he is beginning to understand the "why" to his behaviors. Through the experience of feelings, he moves to a more insightful cognitive position that can only truly be made after having felt what he *needed* to feel. I believe that feelings are the energizers for our outlook on, and behavior in, life. That the energy, or feeling, must be experienced to be understood is basic to the therapeutic process. The energy is experienced on many different levels. It can be initially internal—such as thoughts, but it must eventually become external. The energy comes out verbally or nonverbally. Nonverbal expression can be in body language, writing (which is a close neighbor to verbalization), physical exertion, art, and perhaps most significantly—through the playing (improvisation) of music. Once expressed, there is a need to understand the function of the emotions. They can be looked at in relationship to the behavior, and decisions can be made regarding the feelings and the behavior. Feelings that are *not felt/expressed* tend to gain more energy over time. This holding in or penting up of emotional expression offsets the equilibrium of an individual—and therefore expression is extremely important. The Middle Stage of treatment is crucial to the eventual progression of the client not only through the treatment regime, but also through life. This stage concludes with decisions about oneself—how to move into the future.

4. *Late*: In the late stage, the client begins to look at all that has been accomplished and how to apply it to his life after being discharged from the treatment facility. He must formulate plans and make decisions. There is anxiety at times about leaving a place that he has found as being "safe." He might "act out" a bit to help sever a sense of emotional reliance on the facility. It is a time of trying to find resolution to all problems, which is unrealistic. What he must leave with are skills, strategies, and a plan for the continuing efforts in recovery.

5. *Post-Treatment*: The ability to follow through is the central focus of post-treatment. The plans that were laid must now be acted upon with consistency if success is to be realized and maintained. Whether it is staying on the medicine, participating in outpatient therapy or groups, journal writing, or any other host of treatments, the client must now take a very real sense of responsibility for his own well being and growth.

REFERENCES

Aalberg, P. (1990). *Montana half light.* Various artists—Windham Hill: the first ten years. Stanford, CA: Windham Hill Records.

Bandler, R. & J. Grinder (1975). *The structure of magic. I: A book about language and therapy.* Palo Alto, CA: Science and Behavior Books.

Bandler, R. & J. Grinder (1979*). Frogs into princes: neurolinguistic programming.* Moab, UT: Real People Press.

Bandler R., and J. Grinder (1982). *Reframing.* Moab, UT: Real People Press.

Bandler, R. & J. Grinder, J. (1981). *Trance-formations: neuro-linguistic programming and the structure of hypnosis.* Moab, UT: Real People Press.

Beck, A. (1970). "Cognitive therapy: Nature and relation to behavior therapy." *Behavior Therapy* 1, pp. 184–200.

Beck, A. (1976). *Cognitive therapy and the emotional disorders.* New York: International Universities Press.

Cautela, J. R. (1976). "The present status of covert modeling." *Journal of Behavior Therapy and Experiential Psychiatry* 6, 323–326.

Chapdelaine, M. (1995). *With love.* Richmond, VA: Time-Life.

Chapman, T. (1988). *Tracy Chapman.* New York: Elektra

Cormier, W. H., & L. S. Cormier (1985). *Interviewing strategies for helpers: Fundamental skills and cognitive behavioral interventions.* 2nd. Ed. Monterey, CA: Brooks/Cole.

Corsini, R. J. (Ed.) (1977). *Current personality theories.* Itasca, IL: F. E. Peacock.

Ellis, A. (1984). *Rational emotive-therapy and cognitive behavior therapy.* NewYork: Springer.

Ellis, A. (1962). *Reason and emotion in psychotherapy.* New York: Lyle Stuart.

Freed, B. (1987). "Songwriting with the chemically dependent." *Music Therapy Perspectives* 4, pp. 13–19.

Gabriel, P. (1992). *Us.* Los Angeles, CA: Geffin Records.

Gilliland, B., R. James & J. Bowman (1989). *Theories and strategies in counseling and psychotherapy.* 2nd Ed. Englewood Cliffs, NJ: Prentice Hall.

Lippin, R. A. (1983). "Poetry and poetry therapy: A conversation with Aurthur Lerner." *Journal of arts in Psychotherapy* 9(3), pp. 167–174.

Meichenbaum, D. H. (1977). *Cognitive behavior modification: An integrative approach.* New York: Plenum.

Plach, T. (1980). *The creative use of music in group therapy.* Springfield, IL: Charles C. Thomas.

Saliers, E. (1990). *Nomads, saints, indians—Indigo Girls.* New York: CBS Records.

Springsteen, B. (1975). *Born to run.* New York: CBS Records.

Wilcox, D. (1989). *How did you find me here.* Hollywood, CA: A&M Records

Chapter 12

GROUP VIGNETTE: WORDS AND MUSIC

*The more I know, the less I understand. All the things I thought I
knew, I'm learning again. I'm trying to get down to the heart of the
matter, but my will gets weak and my thoughts seem to scatter—But
I think it's about forgiveness . . .*

—Don Henley (The Heart of the Matter)

CLINICAL SETTING

The clients that are involved in this vignette are all part of a
chemical dependency recovery program as also described in
Chapter 5. The program is a twelve-step-based program. The
clients are living in an unlocked group environment. They are
involved in various lectures and groups throughout the day. Music
therapy is held in a separate building, and a staff member escorts
the clients to the session. The clients that are part of this group are
at various levels in their recovery.

THE CLIENTS

Bert—A white 33-year-old married man who comes from a
wealthy family in upstate New York. His issues in growing up
were that his parents were emotionally unavailable to him and that
they were alcoholics. He came into treatment because of his sexual
addiction to pornography. He is a college graduate but currently
unemployed. He has been in this treatment program for 25 days,
and this is his first music therapy group.

Mikey—A white 45-year-old male who is recently divorced
and has a dependency on alcohol. He has expressed a great deal of
sadness about his failed relationship. He was married for nineteen
years and has four children. The history of his childhood is
relatively unremarkable and has stated that he had grown up in a

fairly normal environment. He has been in the treatment program for a week and this is his first music therapy group.

Darcy—A white 28-year-old single female who is dependent on drugs and alcohol. At the age of 16, drug dealers raped her. Her parents were emotionally abusive, and she reports strong verbal abuse by her father. She also gets into physical altercations with male companions. Lately, she has become very suicidal and depressed. She has had several arrests for driving under the influence—the last one really precipitated the current hospitalization. She has been in the treatment center for 1 week and this is her second music therapy group.

Candy—A white-28-year-old stripper with a history of bipolar disorder, substance abuse, post traumatic stress from early sexual abuse, and also suffers from bulimia. She attempted suicide six months prior to this admission cutting her arms with a knife. She is unmarried with a 3-year-old daughter. She has been in the treatment center for one week and this is her first music therapy group.

The group enters and a mental health worker accompanies them. I am improvising on guitar fairly slow, relaxing tones. I quickly scan the group and realize that most of them have not been in my group before. I invite them to come in and sit, either on a pillow or a chair. They all decide to sit on pillows around the quartz bowl. As they sit, I continue to play and welcome them to the music therapy group today. I put my guitar in its case and begin.

THE SET UP

This session primarily consists of listening to songs, reading the lyrics, and discussing what has been heard. I have the lyrics typed and prepared for all the songs that will be listened to on that that day. Since I also treat the session much like a class learning situation, I also have a chalkboard or a dry erase board available.

This vignette is centered on the theme of stages of hospitalization (or treatment) that a client goes through. The songs that are used will reflect different stages of hospitalization. I have a specific sequence of songs I use that has modified over the years. Below is a listing of all the songs that I have used since I developed this group intervention:

> "Doctor Man"—Livingston Taylor
> "Gentleman"—Livingston Taylor
> "Doctor My Eyes"—Jackson Browne
> "Love to Be Loved"—Peter Gabriel
> "Leaf in A Whirlwind"—Robert Hutto (Unpublished)
> "Montana Half Light"—Philip Aaberg (piano instrumental)
> "Beau Fleuve"—Michael Chapdelaine (classical guitar instrumental)
> "Watershed"—Emily Saliers
> "I Dreamed a Dream"—from "Les Miserables" by A. Boublil and C. M. Schonberg

For the following vignette I used the compact disc format of the following songs in the order presented:

> "Love To Be Loved"—Peter Gabriel
> "Montana Half Light"—Philip Aaberg
> "Watershed"—Emily Saliers

I begin by improvising on the classical guitar as the group enters the room. I also will use my own improvisation near the end of the group, which not only will have an immediate purpose at that time, but also add a nice sense of balance to the overall group. I have a 14-inch quartz toning bowl in the center of the room surrounded by large pillows and comfortable chairs outside of the pillows.

THE SESSION

Beginning—Warm up

Ron   Well . . . I see some new faces this week. (I go around the group and introduce myself to each person.) Welcome to

	my group! This is music therapy and as you probably already surmise—this is a little different from some of the things you've been involved with. I've met you all, and just to remind you, my name is Ron. I do groups here on a contract basis. When I am not here, I am teaching at Cal State Northridge where I am in charge of the Music Therapy Program.
Bert	You can get a degree in music therapy?
Ron	Yep! We even have a Certification process and have to renew our certification every five years.
Bert	I never heard of it!
Ron	Well, we've been around for a long time . . . anyway, in music therapy we do a lot of different types of groups. Sometimes, we play instruments like those you see behind me. Sometimes, we get involved in imagery work—kind of like dream work. Last week, when Darcy was here, we put together a story . . . a group myth inspired by music that we were listening too. From the story we learned a little about our own journey in treatment.
Darcy	Yeah, it was really cool!
Ron	It was pretty neat . . .
Darcy	It was really amazing how we all worked together with our images . . .and how you were able to help us find the symbolism in it all . . . it was so cool.
Ron	Thanks . . . well, like I've said, we do many different types of things in music therapy. Before we get started, I'd like to just kind of get an idea where everyone is at today . . . how things are going.
Darcy	Well I'm doing better than last week, but I've had a pretty emotional day. I've been dealing with a lot of stuff in group . . . that's about it.
Ron	OK . . .
Mikey	I've been OK today, nothing really much happening, just trying to get into the program.
Bert	Well . . . things are going along just fine I think, that's about it. Are we going to be playing anything today?
Ron	I'm not sure just yet . . . do you want to play instruments?

Bert	No, not really . . .
Ron	Well, we'll just see . . . Candy? You look a little tired.
Candy	I want to go to sleep. They woke me up to come here . . . I just want to sleep.
Ron	Do you feel a need to go back, or do you think you can try to make it through the group?
Candy	No . . . I'm going to stay.
Ron	OK.

After quickly assessing the group, I notice there is no real talk of feelings, except a little from Darcy. I decide to go with what I call the "Doctor" group. The reason is that the group is all in early to middle stages of treatment. I think that they might be able to begin to open up more regarding feelings, goals, and thoughts they are having by initially focusing on the external stimulus of lyrics and music. I have found that this is an excellent way to get people to talk about themselves. They first project onto the lyrics, and then the group helps them in owning their feelings at a later time in the group.

Ron	You see in the center of the room a 100% quartz crystal bowl. It is a toning bowl that gives off the pitch of "B." I like to begin the music therapy groups with a gathering around the bowl, as it has powerful vibrations. When you put your hands up by it like this . . . you can feel the energy come into your body. So I invite you to come up near it and as you experience the tone, take a few slow deep breaths and let yourself find some comfort in the experience. (They gather around the bowl, and I begin playing it, at first at a low dynamic where I observe their physical reaction to the sound. I make sure that no one is having an adverse reaction. I do this for about a minute to a minute and a half.)
Darcy	Isn't that neat.
Bert	I want one!
Mikey	That's great!

I notice that although Candy has come up by the bowl, she looks very lethargic, and after a few moments she slouches against the wall with her eyes barely open. As the tone dissipates, I begin speaking—at first my volume level is low—matching the dynamic of the bowl. I then slowly raise my dynamic. This is a good way of making a transition from the feeling that has been established with the tone, back to one that is more verbal. I do not break the mood drastically, but rather come from it to another.

Ron	The session we're going to be involved with today is one of my favorite music therapy activities. It is pretty easy in that you just get to sit back, listen to some songs and talk about them.
Bert	That sounds easy enough!
Ron	Listening is pretty easy . . . (note the NLP strategy of tying in Bert's saying "sounds" and my reply of "listening"). Before we start, I need to give you some background on how this group is structured. First of all, I want you all to imagine for a moment that instead of being here in a treatment program, that you are the doctors or therapists in charge of the treatment program . . . take a second and imagine that switch, imagine having the title of "Doctor" before your name . . . Have any of you seen *"One Flew Over The Cuckoo's Nest?"*
Mikey	We were just talking about that today . . . kind of how we all feel like we're in that movie!
Ron	You know the part where Jack Nicholson escapes with some patients to a marina, and they are just about to steal a boat when a security officer stops them and asks who they are. Jack states that they are from the state hospital. The security officer gets a puzzled look on his face, and Jack quickly says, not to get the wrong idea, that they are all actually physicians from the hospital. He then goes on to introduce each member of his part with the prefix "Doctor" so and so!
Bert	Yeah . . . that part is so funny.
Ron	And as he introduces them, the camera does a close up on their faces. With each close up, you say to yourself

"Well, yeah, he looks like a doctor!" So, as I look around the room at each of you, I can see you as Doctor Mikey, Doctor Bert, Doctor Candy, and Doctor Darcy.

(The group all look at each other, some are quietly laughing, others smiling.)

Ron   So, we've established that you are all now the psychiatrist, and since this is my group, I am the head psychiatrist! I am going to review some things that you learned in med school . . . just to refresh your memory. (I go to the dry erase board and draw the following.)

Pre/Crisis	Early	Mid
Late	Post	

Ron   I'm sure you all remember the various stages of treatment a client goes through when they are interned in a treatment facility.

Bert   Well, good Doctor Ron, I seemed to be a bit rusty in that area, could you review it for us? (The group laughs.)

Ron   Precisely my intention my good man! Before a client actually enters a treatment program, there is usually some sort of crisis that precipitates the admission. Remember the client may or may not be in therapy at the time of the crisis. Something usually happens where a decision is made by either the client, the client's family, or society, that the client needs to be in a program.

At this point in time, I am watching the body responses of the clients, I can already see that many of them are nodding. I have learned that they are often recollecting their own experience of crisis and admission.

Ron   That leads us to the next stage—Early. In the Early stage the clients are beginning to adjust to the program. They are meeting new people, new therapists, and looking for some grounding and momentary resolution from the crisis. They may or may not be understanding why they are there. The next stage is the Middle stage, where the client begins to get in touch with feelings. They are also searching for and eventually finding answers and reasons for their behavior and the relationship with feelings. This may be a most difficult time of treatment because of working through painful issues and possibly confronting people or ideas that have been issues for them. As they work through the middle stage, they move into the Late stage. In the Late stage, they are preparing for discharge. The clients are at a point where they must reenter society. The Post stage is when the client re-enters society and then maintains the behaviors or skills that he learned in the process. They are doing follow up counseling, going to meetings, staying on their medication; they are basically doing what they need to do to continue on their road of recovery. Are there any questions?

Darcy	So the middle stage is where they are working through feelings? Is that right?
Ron	Yes, it is a stage where the client must be willing to experience feelings, talk about them, and try to work through them in a cognitive fashion. Any other questions at this time? No? . . . OK. Let's set up the scenario now. You are the psychiatrist, you are in your office when the client comes in for a session. What is the first thing that you would say to them?
Bert	What's going on?
Darcy	How are you feeling today?
Ron	Those are good answers, but really the first question might be . . . what kind of insurance do you have? (The group all laughs . . . I notice that Candy is seemingly paying more attention. She was slouched against the wall reclining on some large cushions, and now she has begun to take a more sitting upright posture.) You do have to get paid, right?
Bert	That's a good one!
Mikey	Yeah, and we're worth a lot!
Bert	You got that right!

Ron	So . . . after you get the formalities out of the way . . . then the question . . . how are things going today? The reply, however, is not what you might expect. Instead of telling you how they are doing, or feeling, they instead say to you that they are unable to verbalize their feelings today, but instead they have brought you some music that they wrote, which describes what they are currently going through. They then hand you a tape and ask you to listen to it. So what you will hear today is that music. As you listen to it, try to decide what stage of treatment they are in. Listen to the words and music, and try to get an understanding of what they are going through, and then decide what stage they might be in.
Candy	Can they be in different stages, or cross stages?
Ron	Good question. Try to keep them to one stage if possible, if you think they are crossing stages, or moving from one to the next, that also may be possible. You are, after all, the doctor and can make these determinations yourself.
Mikey	So we just listen to the music and try to decide where they are in treatment?
Ron	Yeah, it's a fun activity, just listen to what they say . . . and then try to determine if they are in a crisis mode, an early stage, mid, late, or post stage. After each song, we'll discuss it as if in a staffing, where you can justify your placement on this grid. OK? Any more questions? (Everyone looks ready. The beginning or warm up of the group is now transitioning to a middle section where I will take a less verbal role.)

Middle

I pass out the lyrics to the first song—"Love To Be Loved" by Peter Gabriel. The song has a driving beat with a refrain stating, "I love to be loved." It refers to someone who is going through painful changes and seems to be feeling very alone. In the middle of the song, there is a definite change of feeling and music accompaniment. The writer states:

This old familiar craving,
I've been here before—this way of behaving.
Don't know who the hell I'm saving anymore.

Let it pass let it go let it leave,
From the deepest place I grieve,
This time I believe.
And I let go of it.

He continues to state how difficult this is for him and that it is taking all of his strength to go through this process.

Ron   Our first client's name is Peter. So Peter walks into the room and after having the insurance discussion you ask him how he feels today. He says he can't really tell you except through the music he has written. He then hands you a cassette tape, which you are about to hear. I'll give you a little clue to the first song, and something to listen for. In the middle of the song, there is a change of music and perhaps a change of feeling. Listen for it. OK—here we go. (I play the CD.)

(As the song ends Candy raises her hand. She is now sitting more erect and seems more alert.)

Ron   Candy . . . would you like to start?
Candy   Yeah, you said that if we think that he's moving through stages that we can say that . . . right?
Ron   Sure . . .
Candy   OK, this is how I see it. I see him going through just about all the stages in this song, so maybe he's being discharged or relapsing or something.

Here again I key in on the predicate she is using—what representational system she is relating from. She is primarily in the visual system—which signals my response.

Ron   Where do you *see* what stages he is in . . . what lines are you referring to?

Candy   Well, really he's starting in late early at the beginning of the song. Where he says "The fear of letting go." That's in the early stage. But really, I think the most important line is "This old familiar craving, I've been here before this way of behaving." I think that shows his insight into his problem, which I think is drugs.

Whenever clients pick out a very important line for them, I see it as one of the keys to where they might be. I think that the line has a particular resonance for Candy and so I mentally note this as being particularly important.

Candy   This line puts him in the middle stage—it is also where the music really changes, so something must be really happening for him here, it might be his turning point, I don't know . . . But I do believe he makes it through to the end of the late stage by the end of the song.

Ron   So your *perception* of Peter is that he has brought you a song that describes his whole treatment experience?

Candy   Yeah . . . I think that's what it is . . . the whole thing—all the stages.

(I go the dry erase board and go to the last box and write "Other." In the last category box which was previously blank.)

Ron   So we'll state that a new category is created called "other" where we can put responses that don't exactly fit into the current diagram . . . (I place a 1 in this box with Candy's name next to it.) This is to indicate that Candy put the first client here—and this is client number one. OK . . . someone else?

I indicate which stage the client puts the song on the board along with their name next to it. In this particular instance, Candy has not followed the directions exactly. This is fine with me as it is what Candy is offering to me at this time. This leaves room for variance within this particular session. The patients watch as the session progresses to see where they put the majority of their songs. It also makes for a nice point of discussion after each song is finished—where the majority of he group places the song. I also think that by writing it on the board—much like a classroom or learning situation, it keeps the clients focused on looking at the chart.

Mikey   Well I put him moving from early to mid.

(This, by the way, is where the majority of clients put this song. I place a number one (1) in the Early category with an arrow next to it leading to Middle. I also put Mikey's name by it.)

Mikey   The change of the music really caught my attention, but the words were also very powerful there. When he sings, "Let it pass, let it go, let it leave, from the deepest place I grieve, this time I believe—and I let go." That tells me he is in some real pain and having a real hard time getting through this. From what you've said, that is what happens in the middle stage. But there is one thing that I can't get . . . and that is the line "I cannot face the cost." I just can't get what that means . . .

Candy   Maybe he's just not ready to deal with it all.

Mikey   I don't know—there's something about that line . . .

At this point—I can see that Mikey is doing some introspection . . . so the question arises do we stop and work on that one line with him, or do we continue with the group and see if it starts coming together for him as the group progresses. I decide to continue. I do, however, make a mental note of this for later.

Darcy   I think he's in the middle also. The part that gets me is when he says "I'm losing such a central part of me." (Darcy sits quietly for a few moments.)

Ron   That's the *part* that's important for you? (I put a number one in the Middle category with Darcy by it.)

Darcy   Yeah . . . to get out of his addiction he's got to lose some things that are not good for him to move forward . . . but those things that he is losing have been a part of him for a long time. So . . . he must lose a little to hopefully win big later.

Again, I am thinking that this is really relating to her own situation, especially since she said "hopefully." Since there will be time for introspection and tying everything together at the end of the session, I decide to move on to Bert.

Ron	Bert, what did you think?
Bert	Well, I think the song covers the whole gamut of treatment. (I place a 1 in the "Other" category with Bert's name by it.) The first two lines are when he is in pre-treatment or in a crisis—he's in "darkness"—doesn't seem to know what's going on around him. Then—in Early treatment he's in primal pain—he's crying like a baby—no thinking involved—just experiencing pain . . . when babies cry . . . they don't think about why they are crying . . . they are just crying—because they are in pain. He moves to mid at the music change—the familiar craving part. He then goes into late by letting go and realizing he has lost part of himself and is ready to return to the real world. Part of recognizing the loss is also trying to figure out how he is now going to cope with everything he has to return to.
Candy	That's it! You hit it on the head.
Bert	Yeah—but he's also a narcissist . . . needing to be loved all the time, not being able to give it—the whole focus is on himself . . . he's a narcissist.

The whole time Bert is talking, I notice the tone in his voice, very calculating, without much feeling. He is very analytical in his manner toward the song. He does not show any outward signs like the others that the song has had any effect on him at all. I am beginning to think that he is identifying and projecting his own narcissistic traits onto the lyrics.

Ron	That's quite an analysis.
Bert	Yeah, I needed to pull out my pen and take notes while it

was going on so I wouldn't forget my thoughts.

Ron   You said them quite well. Before we move on to the next song, take a moment and look again at the lyrics. Find a line or two that, for you, really tells you where the client is currently at. You know, when you are talking to your therapist, he will often key into a few phrases that seem to have great deal of emotional attachment for you. He might then bring you back to those phrases from time to time for clarification of your feelings and thoughts. So . . . pick out a line or two that you think are important.

Candy   Do you mean that is important—or meaningful for us, or the patient?

This was a wonderful comment, it shows how Candy is already quite involved and having a hard time separating herself from the music and words.

Ron   Being the doctor, it is something that you feel had a great amount of emotion in it as it was being sung by the client—the whole song might be emotionally charged, but try to find one or two lines that you feel are the most charged . . . OK?

I let them review the song as I prepare the next disc. I am also thinking of Bert and his comments. As I said, he was quite analytical and at times "matter of fact" sounding as he spoke of the song. The only time he appeared as if there was emotional involvement was when he was calling the client a narcissist. He repeated it a few times and was quite emphatic about this point after Candy responded to his analysis.

Ron   OK . . . you all did quite well in that analysis.

Bert   Who was right?

Ron   Well, the opinions all were said with such confidence, I can't really tell you who had the correct answer.

Mikey   Is there a correct answer?

Ron   Maybe . . . maybe not . . . you'll need to be patient till the end of the session to see . . . OK? So . . . let's move on to the second selection. The second client's name is Philip. He comes into your office, and being a well prepared psychiatrist, you have a piano in the office!! Philip sits down at the piano, and he tells you this is what he is feeling today. He plays, but there are no words to this one, just Philip playing the piano. So . . . you must listen closely to the music and hear what it is saying to you . . . if you wish you can close your eyes . . . OK? Here's Philip

(I play the CD of "Montana Halflight" by Philip Aaberg. It is solo acoustic piano, which has, for the most part a ostinato or repeating bass line accompaniment, a lyrical melody, and an overall serene feel. In the middle of the piece, there is a musical change where the tempo gets a bit quicker, and there is an obvious harmonic sound of tension. It nicely resolves then to the beginning feeling, and in fact, the beginning is repeated. As the piece ends, Candy again raises her hand and wants to be first to comment.)

Candy   I see him as being caught in denial—somewhere between crisis and the early stage.

Ron   So he *appears* to be in denial? (I mark a number 2 on the board under Pre and Early with Candy's name by it.)

This is the first time I had ever heard such a response—denial. Most clients put this piece in the post category. I'm beginning to think that Candy is projecting quite strongly at this point in time.

Candy   Yeah . . . he wants to keep every thing away from him and not go any place in his treatment. He's caught—he can't face his problems.

Ron   I *see* . . . someone else?

Bert   It sounded to me like a whole program again. It's a journey where he goes through treatment, and that one part where there is a crescendo, that is the part where he has to make changes in his life. Then he gets out of treatment and just cruises through life.

Ron   Cruises?

Bert	Yeah . . . you know, he's got the whole thing pretty much worked out. He is staying with his program, he's keeping it together . . .
Ron	OK . . . Cruises. (I mark a number 2 on the board under "Other" with Bert's name by it.)

Bert's voice and demeanor are quite strong at this point. I keep going back in my mind to the narcissistic comment. Also, in both songs he doesn't pick just one stage, but has the song moving through all the stages—passive aggressive behavior.

Mikey	Well I thought it was post. It sounded mellow to me, that is how post should be, mellow. Then when there was that crescendo—as Bert called it—that was when a problem would come up that he had to work through. The calm part comes back again because he works through the problem. That's how it's supposed to be in Post.
Ron	Good . . . nicely said. Darcy, what about you?
Darcy	I think it is Late moving into Post. The one part where it sounds agitated and a little louder, that is the anxiety and apprehension of getting discharged and having to go back into the big mean world out there.
Ron	What comes after the agitation?
Darcy	That is making it . . . . you know . . . survival.
Ron	Good, also nicely said. You all have incredible insights to the music. Sometimes this is a difficult one, but you all have really described your thoughts on this one very well.
Bert	Why thank you!
Candy	Music therapy is great! Can we get it every day?
Ron	Bert you are certainly welcome, and, Candy, I wish it was possible to have it every day with you guys, but right now that just can't be worked out . . . are you ready for the last piece? This one is written by Emily. (I hand to them the lyrics to "Watershed" by the Indigo Girls. I then put on the CD.)

This song has many wonderful parts. She speaks in many metaphors throughout the song, which allows for the clients to relate to it in many different and very personal ways. The song seems to speak of many struggles she has gone through and is now reflecting on her life process and the choices she has made. Below is the chorus:

> *Up on the watershed, standing at the fork in the road*
> *You can stand there and agonize*
> *Till you agony's your heaviest load.*
> *You'll never fly as the crow flies, get used to a country*
>   *mile.*
> *When you're learning to face the path at your pace*
> *Every choice is worth your while.*

Ron	Who would like to start?
Bert	I will. This woman is a mess! She's done it all but seems like she hasn't really learned a thing. I definitely feel that she is in a relapse. (I am marking a number 3 under the "Other" category and placing Bert's name by it.) She starts off by saying she really doesn't know herself at all—"Thought I knew my mind like the back of my hand." She knows that this relapse and treatment are going to be difficult for her. In the chorus, she continues to be confused and making things more difficult, and it seems that we don't know if she comes to a decision or not. Then the line, "Well there's always retrospect to light a clearer path. Every five years or so I look back on my life and have a good laugh." And then she says, "But ending up where I started makes me wanna stand still." That's where I hear her saying that she really is not making gains in her life . . . she keeps getting caught in patterns that are hurtful to her. So . . . I definitely think she is in a relapse mode.
Candy	Again, I am kind of with you Bert. The part of the "twisted guard rail and the broken glass on the cement," I think is symbolic for her own crack up. And then she says she needs to "starve the emptiness and feed the hunger," which I think is her own loneliness, and to feed the hunger is her hunger to live! (I write the number 3 in the "Other" category with Candy's name on it.)
Bert	That's great, Candy.

Candy   Thanks . . . but I'm not finished. I see her falling into the relapse also with the verse of looking back and also feeling like she is standing still. She's not learned anything from all this pain . . . and I think that is sad.

As she is saying this last statement, I notice that her voice is a little less present and she seems to be withdrawing within herself. It seems that as she said those last words, she also saw a part of her own life, which has so much pain in it, and she is in resonance with the sadness of the words she read.

Ron   It *looks* like you understand this song and client pretty well . . .

Candy   I just see her as being a victim of her own foolishness, not being able to change. But she also has obstacles to overcome. The part of the guard rail and broken glass, I think that part is symbolic of very hard obstacles that fall into your path. I can really see these things as obstacles.

Ron   You seem to have good *insight* . . . you are very *perceptive.*

Candy   Thank you . . . I've said enough . . . someone else can talk.

Darcy   I think also that she is in an early stage of relapse and has done the program before. That's really about it . . . (I write the number 3 in the Early stage with Darcy's name by it.)

Mikey   Well I have a different opinion from everyone. I think she's right smack dab in the middle of middle. She is obviously struggling with her feelings and decisions she has to make in her life. She is confused in a way that I wouldn't put her in the Early stage. I think she is beyond that. I do think that she is trying to figure out why she is the way she is. So I put her in the middle. (I write the number 3 in the Middle stage with Mikey's name by it.)

Ron   Thanks Mikey, those are also excellent insights . . . Before we continue, just look back through the song and like the first song, find a line or two that you think is more emotionally charged than the others. A line that

	really describes for you where the client is at . . . OK . . .
Bert	So who was right?
Ron	We're not quite at that point yet, Bert, but we're getting close to the end of the session. Before we wrap it up today, there is a little exercise that I would like you to do. Why don't you get as comfortable as you can with the large pillows. (I pick up my guitar.) I invite you to close your eyes . . . I am going to summarize today's music therapy session for you and also play a little music for you.

As I begin to play, I reflect on the whole group. I remember certain answers from the group and similarities in content of the many comments. This kind of tells me where the group is as whole, as well as individual members. Most of the group has not been in treatment a long period of time. The answers were, for the most part, very well said and thoughtful.

Ron	Concentrate for a moment on your breath . . . let it slow down . . . let each breath be a little longer than the last . . . let each breath fill your whole upper body, not just your chest, let each one be deep . . . (I give time for this.) Think back to when you walked into the room, reflect back on your first thoughts . . .

I first help them relax through some breathing exercises. I then take them to a reality-based image of coming in the room. I try to ground them there with their comments and feelings. I then invite them to do some active imagery for future action, based on the concepts they learned from the group as well as the feelings that may have been clarified for them through this group activity. All the while, I am improvising a slow melodic pattern. The bass is rich and full, and is slowly repetitive in nature. With each of the following questions or suggestions, there is a pace of saying the words, which is not too quick, but flowing with the music being improvised in the background. There is varied and leisurely amount of time between each statement.

Ron   Think of your reactions to the first song . . . think of the line that was most important for you . . . think of the piano music of the second song . . . can you imagine the feelings you had as you listened to it? . . . Remember what you said about it? . . . Think of the last song . . . think of the lines that were important for you . . . think of why they might be of importance for you . . . Now, if you were your own doctor, which we all eventually are, where would you place yourself on the chart . . . Early . . . Middle . . . . Late . . . where would you place yourself. In order for you to get to the next stage, what would you have to do? . . . Can you imagine yourself doing what you need to do to get to the next stage? . . . Can you *see* yourself doing what needs to be done? . . . Can you *hear* yourself in your mind's ear saying what needs to be done? . . . Can you *feel* the need to move forward? . . . Just spend a little time now *imagining* success and what it *feels* like in moving to the next stage . . .

I state the questions in three different sensory representational systems as described in NLP. My hope is that the clients key into the phrase that most stimulates them to be successful in this little exercise.

End

Ron   OK . . . we're going to come back in just a minute. Before we do and before you leave, we're going to close the group with having you verbalize to the group the stage you think you are in and how you think you can get to the next stage . . . Slowly start waking up your body now . . . perhaps you might want to wiggle your fingers and toes . . . take some deep breaths . . . just start coming back and then come sit in a circle around the bowl.

(Everyone slowly gets up and comes and sits in a circle around the crystal bowl.)

Ron   Now that everyone's back . . . let me tell you how we're

going to end our session today . . . I'd like to end the
music therapy group by passing around this harmony ball.
(I show them the ball and let the chimes in it ring a
couple of times.) We'll pass this around the group, and
when you have it, it is your turn to tell the group what
stage you are in, and what you need to do to get to the
next stage . . . OK? (I roll the ball to Candy.)

*I look at Candy and remember how she first looked when she came
into the group, very lethargic, and slumping posture. She is now
sitting erect, much more alert overall, yet with a very pensive look
on her face. I also think of how she began to respond through this
session and how she asked how many times a week she would be
able to be involved in music therapy. This question come up often
in my groups as I imagine it does in many other music therapy
groups.*

Candy	Whew . . . (Long pause as she listens to the chimes of the harmony ball in her hand.) You know . . . I've been in therapy for so long . . . I'm so sick of it . . . and right now I am in the Early stage, wishing I could some how get to the Middle stage. In the third song, I related to the part where I think she had so many obstacles in her way . . . you know on the road to recovery . . . there's just so much crap . . . I don't know where to begin . . .
Ron	So you *see* yourself as being confused right now?
Candy	Yeah . . . I'm just so tired of it all . . .
Ron	It's hard to *see* a light at the end of the tunnel?
Candy	Yeah . . . so I don't know how to get to the middle stage . . .
Darcy	I know how that feels . . . I feel like I am just getting into the third stage, and in looking back I think I was stuck in early for awhile . . . be patient Candy . . .
Candy	Thanks . . . Darcy knows a lot of what I am going through . . . we were in the same group this morning.
Ron	Sometimes it's hard to *focus* on only one thing . . . but when you can . . . it helps you go to the next . . . it's like building a bridge, you can *see* the whole thing in your

mind and wonder how am I going to build that! Well, you start with the foundation, and sometimes you need to consult others who know how to build bridges to help you. Then as it begins you can really *envision* the whole bridge . . . which takes you from one side of the river to the other . . . do you *see* what I mean?

Candy   Yeah . . . (She continues to listen to the harmony ball . . . she looks up and smiles . . . takes a deep breath and then rolls the harmony ball to Darcy.)

Darcy   (She holds the harmony ball and listens for a few moments as it chimes.) I love this little ball . . . I would really like to get one . . . well . . . this is a pretty easy question for me. I know that I am in the middle stage . . . I am trying to find out why I use alcohol and drugs so much . . . which is painful in itself . . . To get to the late stage I need to really get back to my spirituality . . . I need to be in touch with my higher power and trust my higher power. I want to thank you for last week's group and this one too . . . they have really helped me . . . I wasn't going to come today
 . . . but Bill, you know Bill from last week? He said that I should, that with music therapy you never know what is going to happen . . . but it's usually something that will help you . . . so . . . thank you.

Ron   You're welcome. (Darcy rolls the ball to Mikey.)

Mikey   I've been here about a week, and I also am trying to get into the middle stage. I know that I need to be more open to the whole experience of being here, and I need to start trusting the process . . . Which I have not fully done yet. (He rolls the ball to Bert.)

Bert   (He rolls the harmony ball in his hands for a few moments.) This little ball is really cool! . . . I am in the middle stage preparing for family week. My wife is coming, and it is important for her to understand what is going on with me . . . if she can start understanding my problems, and me. Then I think that there will be some hope for our marriage. So—I'm in the middle.

All through the session I have noticed that Bert has had a certain attitude . . . almost an arrogance and self-absorption. He put all three of the songs in the "Other" category on the board. He has not consistently followed directions, but instead did what he wanted to do. At times during the music, he would put the lyric sheet down and mouth the words of the song. In the middle piece, he was acting as if he was playing the piano in the air with one hand. I remembered his strong statements about narcissism in the first piece. As the session continued, I became more convinced of his narcissistic traits. Since this is my first meeting with him and since we were out of time, the best I could do was to accept this answer and then chart on the behavior shown in the group. I later spoke with his primary therapist who said these traits had been coming out even more profoundly in the last week.

(Bert rolls the ball to me.)

Ron	(I pause a while as I listen to the ball.) Well, first of all, I think you all did great jobs being the doctor. You all have remarkable insight . . . you should try writing your thoughts down—almost like an idea for a song . . . let them sit for a while, go back and look at them, almost as if they were not yours . . . then see where they might fit on the chart . . . then what you might tell the person who wrote the words to help get them to the next stage. I hope to see many of you in the next group . . . it will be different from this one . . . I try to do something a bit different every time . . . so have a good week—work hard! (The group gets up to leave, and many of the members make a few final comments on how they enjoyed the group and got something out of it. As they were almost all out of the room, Bert stuck his head back in the room.)
Bert	Hey, you didn't tell us who was right about what stages these people actually were in!
Ron	You all were right!

Bert   I knew you'd say that!

So did I.

FINAL THOUGHTS

This session is the oldest activity of all the ones described in this book. This particular format has been successful for me for a long time. The key to this type of session, which involves a good deal of dialogue, is to listen. This seems like a simple technique, but the way in which you listen is very important. Listening to words such as predicates and lines that are meaningful for the client helps in understanding their frame of reference. Listen to their body language—is it in tune with what they say? Trying to hear their melody, timbre, and rhythm. This style of listening is an art.

Letting clients discuss lyrics and music appears easy. But I have seen younger therapists and students fall into the trap of arguing with clients over the meaning of the words. As I have said so many times in this book, what they give you is what they offer, you must receive it for what it is. For the client—it may be who they are.

So listen.

Chapter 13

POSTLUDE

Many are asking, "Who can show us any good?"

—Psalm 4:6

I love what I do. I have been blessed with the opportunity to use one of the most precious gifts on this Earth, music, to help others. I was once asked what the difference was between Music Performance and Music Therapy. My reply came without much thought, there is no real difference if the giver of the music is true to the music. The goal in each is to have a change in the listeners' behavior, cognition, and emotion.

Music does not lie. It is there, almost like a truth serum. The power that it has to stimulate human emotions is awesome. This power lies in its inherent verity and simplicity. It was born out of man's need to communicate and express in a new medium. It has been handed down as part of our inherent human structure for centuries and therefore, even in utero, it is familiar. It has helped the "walls come down" in fact and in symbol.

Music Therapy is an age-old profession. The transformation of it as a profession has been radical and yet unchanging. The physicians, who used music in the tribes of old, were respected healers that had a magical quality about them. They were called upon for all ailments, both physical and mental. They brought with them their drums and their rattles, their chants, stories, songs, herbs, and Presence. They engaged and treated those who were ill, actively involving them in ceremony when appropriate. Then, something happened for the ones who were sick—they began to get better. They began to get better not because of one specific treatment, but because of all that they had experienced. A holistic approach with music was an integral part of the entire process.

The ceremony of today has often too much to do with mere words. Words cannot begin to describe the indescribable emotions of joy and sorrow. The energy of these emotions transfigured into musical sounds may be the only way to really express and understand the emotion. Music *is* the language of emotion. Music is the means by which two strangers can build a relationship that is built on not words, but on trusting in the sounds they exchange. In today's ceremony, now called treatment or therapy, music is again being more widely recognized for its therapeutic effect. Music is ritual, it is powerful, it is spiritual, and it is healing.

As I read over the vignettes, I realize that things could have and often do progress differently in the sessions described. I could have said less or more, been less directive at times or go off on tangents. But these vignettes stand for what they are, moments in time I tried to capture for you.

In writing this book, I have had different music playing in the background much of the time. Some of the music I would play repeatedly for days, and it no longer became background, it became my companion in this writing adventure. I could always count on the melody and harmony, the timbre, rhythm and form. When I tired, it would embrace me and help me rest. When typing in frenzy, it would help me slow down and find clarity. When I needed to move forward, it would change in some fashion and give me a push. It, along with prayer, has been my "flashlight" for finding my way to bring these vignettes and thoughts to you.

I end these writings with a song—a Psalm of David. David may indeed have been the first Music Therapist, for in the psalms he composed you can find much of the essence of healing. This one is special for me in that I feel it captures spirituality and in a tangential fashion, Music Therapy in its verse. So . . . I offer it to you.

> *Many are asking, "Who can show us any good?"*
> *Let the light of your face shine on us, O Lord.*
> *You have filled my heart with greater joy than when the*
> *   grain and the new wine abound.*
> *I will lie down and sleep in peace, for you alone,*
> *O Lord, make me dwell in safety.*